BAR CHORDS
FOR
BEGINNERS

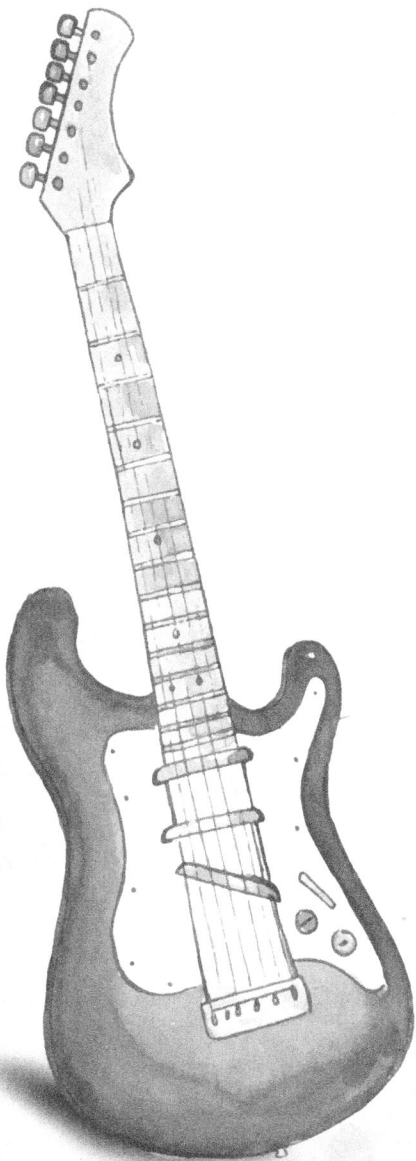

14-day boot camp to overcome the fear of bar chords, play clear-sounding chords with less strain and conquer the songs you skipped

GUITAR HEAD

✉ gh@theguitarhead.com
© ⨍ /theguitarhead

Disclaimer

Dedication

---

*We dedicate this book to the complete
Guitar Head team,
supporters, well-wishers and
the Guitar Head community.*

*It goes without saying that we
would not have gotten
this far without
your encouragement,
critique and support*

Table of Contents

Free Guitar Head Bonuses

Audio Files

All Guitar Head books come with audio tracks for the licks inside the book. These audio tracks are an integral part of the book - they ensure you are playing the charts and chords the way they are intended to be played.

Lifetime Access To Guitar Head Community

Being around like-minded people is the first step to being successful at anything. The Guitar Head community is a place where you can find people who are willing to listen to your music, answer your questions or talk anything guitar.

Email Newsletters Sent Directly To Your Inbox

We send regular guitar lessons and tips to all our subscribers. Our subscribers are also the first to know about Guitar Head giveaways and holiday discounts.

Free PDF

Guitar mastery is all about the details! Getting the small things right and avoiding mistakes that can slow your guitar journey by years. So, we wrote a book about 25 of the most common mistakes guitarists make and decided to give it for free to all Guitar Head readers.

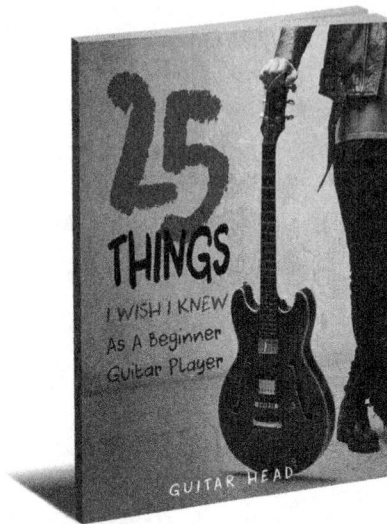

You can grab a copy of the free book, the audio files and subscribe to the newsletter by following the link below.

All these bonuses are a 100% free, with no strings attached. You won't need to enter any personal details other than your first name and email address.

To get your bonuses, go to: ***www.theguitarhead.com/bonus***

Book Profile

Difficulty Level: Beginner

This book is designed to help you learn the essential skills you need to play bar chords confidently all over the fretboard, in all keys, and within progressions.

With the right technique and practice, you'll be playing clear and fatigue-free bar chords in no time.

In addition to mastering bar chords, this book also includes popular chord progressions that utilize bar chords, giving you a wider range of chords to play with.

You'll also learn the CAGED system, which is an efficient way to play bar chords in all keys without having to memorize them.

Technical knowledge you need before reading this book:

To ensure that we maintain focus on bar chords, this book assumes that readers are familiar with beginner-level topics such as:

- » How to hold a guitar and pick.
- » Knowledge of how to read chord charts and tabs.
- » Understanding of basic open chords.
- » Basic understanding of rhythm and strumming techniques.

Suggested reading before this book:

If you are in the 'just got your guitar' phase, we recommend reading the book **"Guitar Chords for Beginners"**

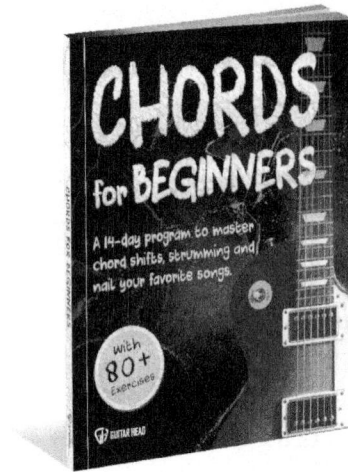

This book offers a structured and motivating approach to learning open chords and chord progressions.

It also covers basic and important topics such as rhythm and strumming techniques, providing a solid foundation for learning bar chords.

INTRODUCTION

I remember the first time I had a close encounter with a B major chord in its natural habitat. I was only a little boy and I had put a huge effort into trying to master open chords. I'm not going to lie, they didn't sound arena-ready, but they were OK.

Yet, the moment I found the B chord I was completely disheartened.

I thought it was an impossible mountain to climb, that I was just "not cut for playing guitar".

If you feel like that too; don't worry, you've come to the right place. Believe me, I have been in your shoes before and I know exactly how you feel and what to do to help you.

Yes, mastering bar chords is, perhaps, the first big challenge every guitarist faces. It's a steep learning curve that we all struggle with. Nevertheless, the ones of us who receive proper guidance and keep practicing end up mastering them.

I'm one of those and I'm here to pass it forward to you.

Yes, I'm going to show you how to master bar chords once and for all in only 14 days. Within two weeks from now, you'll be able to play all those songs you just skipped for that F#m or that B7 in them.

But that's not all, because we're going to go over many chords that will help you grow your musical vocabulary drastically. This will make you not only better at picking up songs by ear but also help you become a better songwriter.

In only 14 days of practice, you'll be able to open up a whole new musical universe and play any and every song you want.

Are you ready to learn bare chords and become the master of your sonic universe?

Get your guitar, because here we go.

Welcome.

What are bar chords?

Barre or bar chords are simply chords that are played by fretting down several strings with our index finger. This is either because they don't include the open-string notes in their formula (can't be played using open strings) or because it is more comfortable to play them with a bar somewhere else on the fretboard.

Bar chords get their name from the simple fact that they are created using our index finger as a bar to press down multiple strings at once.

So, in a nutshell, we could define bar chords as chords that require the player to press down multiple strings at once utilizing the index finger as a bar or capo.

Why Do I Need to Learn Bar Chords?

This is a question I made myself, my teacher, my parents, and the universe multiple times during my early days as a player. Yes, when something stands in the way of your progress as a player you try to find a reason not to do it.

So, to fight back against all the false reasons your mind is coming up with to answer that question with a no, let's take a look at some of the benefits of playing bar chords.

Play Chords That You Can't Play in the Open Position

The first benefit is the one that convinced me in the first place. Yes, the moment you start trying to learn sharp and flat chords, your mind enters a whole new sonic space. Yet, to play those chords, you need to master bar chords first.

Master the bar chords you must, and play sharps and flats you will.

Yoda jokes apart, some chords offer you alternatives to play them where they feel the most comfortable and some others don't. For example, chords as common as F#m or Bb are very intricate unless you play them using bar chords.

Therefore, learning bar chords is paramount to broadening your vocabulary as a player and playing as many songs as you want.

Get a Fuller Sound (Mind the Bass Note)

Nothing sounds bigger than an open chord played with mild overdrive or distortion. If you don't believe me, ask Noel Gallagher about it and he'll tell you a thing or two about the formula that granted Oasis worldwide success.

But how can we make non-open chords sound as big, full, and rich as them? Well, the answer to that question is bar chords. Yes, bar chords are the next biggest-sounding chords after open chords.

This is due to a simple fact: bar chords occupy the entire fretboard and can anchor your tone with that bass root note making it grow enormously. Yes, the vibration of an open string can make a stadium roar with a huge chorus, and your bar chords are the next biggest thing regardless of the chord you're trying to play.

Play Chords in Any Key

A bar chord acts like a capo moving around the guitar's neck. This dynamic version of a capo that you can create with your index finger allows you to transpose any song just like you would do with a capo.

In case you didn't know, when you transpose a song, you change the key respecting the intervals. Hence, as long as you move the same structure up or down tonally, the song will be the same. This is done, for example, to accommodate a song to match a singer's natural vocal register.

Believe me; learning bar chords to pull off this trick will help you avoid the nightmare of forgetting your almighty capo the night of the performance.

Bar Chords are Easy to Remember

The final benefit I'm describing here (the list could go on forever) is that, by learning less than two handfuls of shapes, you can play 90% of the songs in modern Western music. Yes, since you're moving the flesh-made capo around, there is no need to learn chords to use in a particular key. On the contrary, you can use the same shapes in any and all keys.

Furthermore, when you master bar chords, you can play all major, minor, seventh, and minor seventh chords using the same shapes in any section of the fretboard. This makes many songs easier to play since you can choose the chords and positions that feel and sound the best without having to memorize any extra difficult chord shapes.

A 14-Day Journey to Mastery

I set the 14-day rule years ago to teach bar chords to my private students. The number is not at all arbitrary; it is a product of years of teaching young and adult students how to master this important skill. Moreover, we can say that the content you're about to receive is a tested-and-true recipe to play bar chords in 14 days.

Before we start, let me go through two basic FAQs about the 14 days:

» The timeframe is to help you – I indicate a timeframe to learn this valuable skill to help you set a goal and to make sure you can track your progress. If you don't set a time-based goal, you might be wandering in music mist forever. So, this 14-day period shall be your lighthouse in the endless sonic fields of guitar mastery.

» The 14 days are not necessarily consecutive – I know what you're thinking: "I don't have the time to devote 14 consecutive days to learning bar chords, I have a life!" I know you do, and it must be a wonderful one. So, let me give you the good news, you can play as little as 2 days a week and still follow this practice routine successfully.

A New Hope (Don't Give Up!)

I've seen many aspiring guitar players with high hopes and big dreams give it all up because of an F major or a B minor. Furthermore, I've been in their shoes and know what it feels like to have your hands struggle with your brain's orders.

Yes, at first you feel like a juggler having to pay attention to so many things at the same time. Nevertheless, you can do it; you can master bar chords, and once you do, that struggle will be part of the past.

Furthermore, I am here to help you not only learn to master bar chords but also to get rid of the fear and pain associated with them. The fact that the hill is steep doesn't mean you can't conquer it. Plus, on the other side, there is a whole other sonic universe waiting for you to join.

So, you could say this is a book about hope, a book that can help you navigate your path from knowing nothing about bar chords all the way to mastery.

Moreover, we're going to practice, learn songs, and have lots of fun together while you learn one of the main pillars of modern music in terms of chords.

This is where it all begins, join me on this marvelous 14-day trip to bar chord mastery and never look back.

Open Chords Used

I know what you're thinking and yes, you're right, this is a book about bar chords.

That being said, it is a very rare case to find only bar chords in any composition with no open chords to go with them. Yes, open chords are always every guitar player's first choice because they're easy to play and sound huge.

So, we're going to build your knowledge about bar chords starting with the utterly known and all-around amazing open chords.

If you're very familiar with them and, basically, know them inside out, then there's no need to keep reading, you can simply skip to the next chapter.

On the other hand, if you happen to have a somewhat vague idea about open chords, this is the perfect chance to clear all your doubts about them.

Finally, if you have no idea about open chords, reading this chapter is absolutely mandatory for you. Please, read on.

The Open Chords You Need Are These

These are the only open chord shapes you'll have to use for the entire book. Learn to play them inside out and memorize the shapes, they will be very handy later on.

We'll start with major chords, move on to minor chords, and finish with seventh chords.

Without further ado, these are the open chords we need to use for the entire book:

Major Open Chords

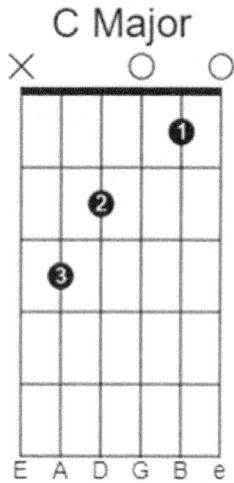

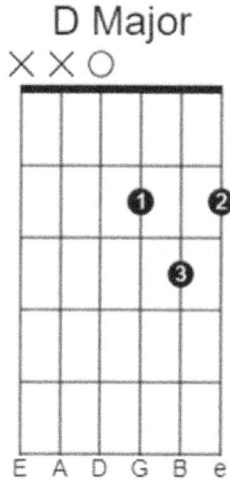

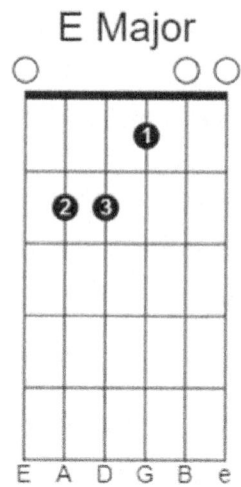

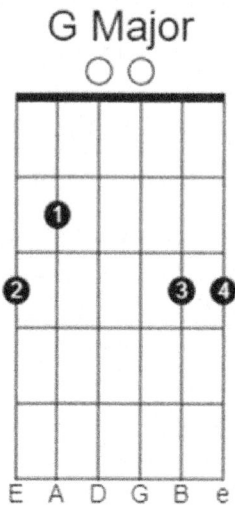

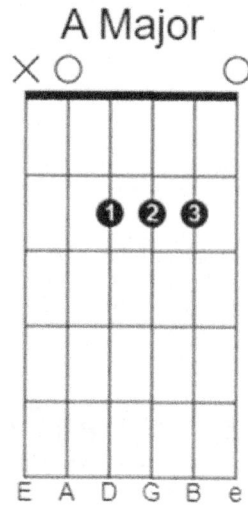

C Major

D Major

E Major

G Major

A Major

Minor Open Chords

D Minor

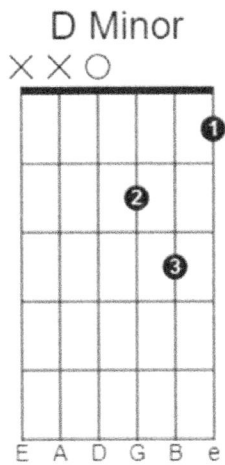

E Minor

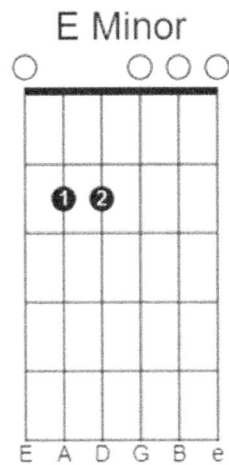

A Minor

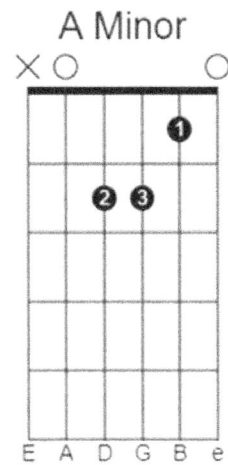

Seventh Open Chords

C 7

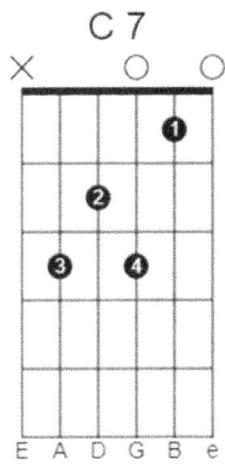

D 7

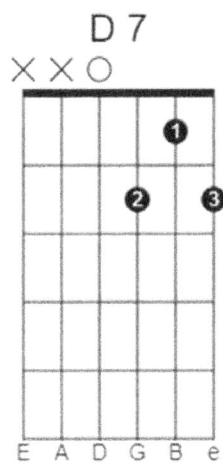

E 7

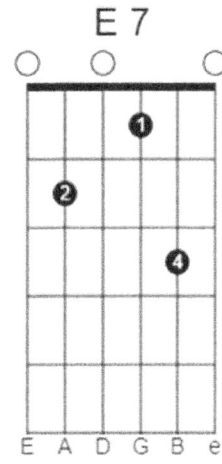

G 7

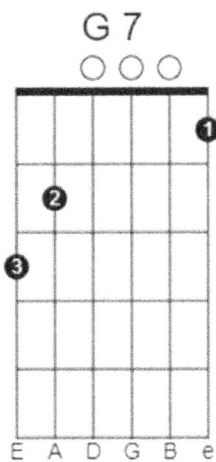

A 7

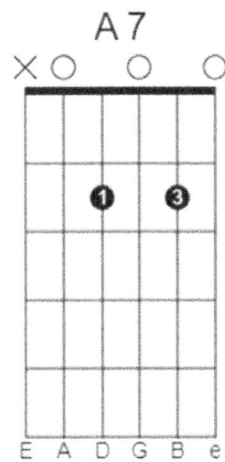

The First
14 DAYS
of Practice

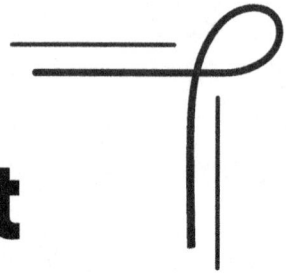

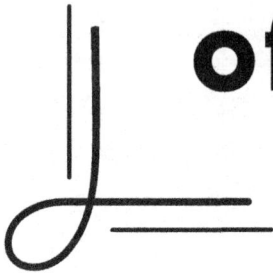

CHAPTER 1

Your First Bar Chord

Welcome to your first day of bar chord training, we will use two days of practice and go through some diagrams in this first chapter. By the end, you should be able to play the B major bar chord understanding the mechanics of the shape and the guitar neck.

Are you ready to take the big first step in the right direction?

Let's do this!

DAY 1

The B Major Chord

In this first approach to playing bar chords properly, we will master the B major chord. We're going to prepare its shape and form it on the fretboard dissecting what part of your hand is doing what. That way, you'll be able to correct any mistakes and misuses right from the very beginning.

Step 1 – Forming the B Major Bar Chord

Our first step is to use the A major shape we have already seen. Play that chord on your guitar; does it sound good? Keep perfecting it until it sounds perfect.

After doing that, the next step is to move that A major shape two frets toward the guitar's bridge and build a B major utilizing the A major structure.

What we'll do is take the root note of the A major chord and turn it into a B. For that, instead of playing the open A string, we'll fret it on the second fret where A turns into B. Next, we'll form an A major shape on the fourth fret. That way, we'll move the same structure from one chord to another.

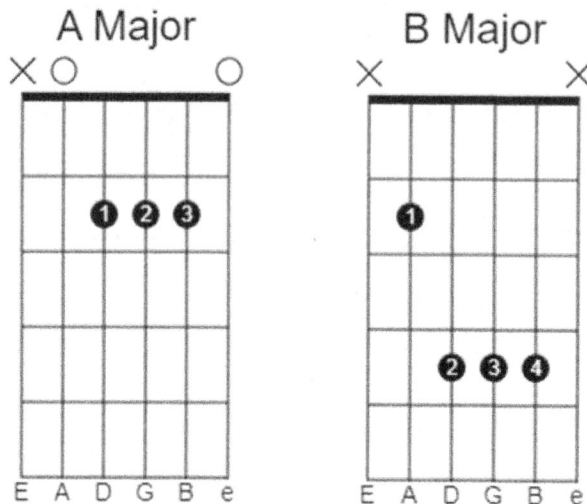

Abstain from playing the 6th and 1st strings on your guitar and make sure you're strumming the four strings in the middle.

How does it sound?

PRO TIP

This is what I call the string-by-string technique; it will help you address every finger separately and solve the issues that are deadening the sound of your chords. So, while holding your first B major chord with the fretting hand, pluck each string individually and find any dead spots.

If you do find any dead spots, just correct that finger's position. Repeat until you have a smooth-sounding chord.

DAY 2

Step 2 – Barring Two Strings at a Time

Your first finger or your index finger is pressing the 5th string second fret. To do this, you have to obligatorily go over the second fret at the 1st string too.

Well, we're going to use that in our favor by playing two extra notes by simply playing them with our index finger.

How do you do this? Well, very simply try to press down the first string with the lower part of your index finger. Pluck it several times until you find your hand's sweet spot and that F# sounds loud and clear.

Once properly placed, the shape looks like this:

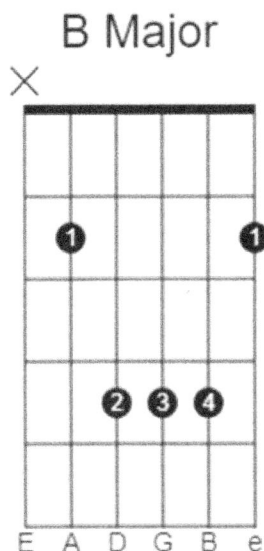

B Major

Now try playing the same while using a full bar that goes from string 1 to string 5. Use the same string-by-string technique to make sure you have no dead sounds.

Just as the diagram indicates, you don't have to pluck the 6th string.

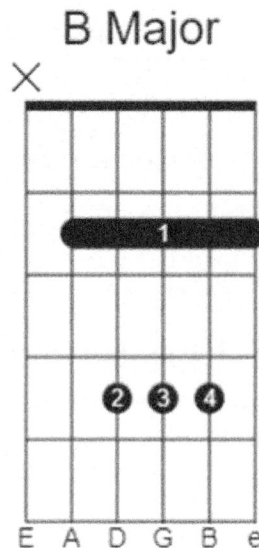

B Major

E A D G B e

Step 3 – The Things to Bear in Mind

In this final step in constructing the B major chord successfully, we'll talk about all the hand movements that you have to bear in mind to construct great-sounding, effortless bar chords anywhere on the fretboard.

I'll give you a few key indicators that are game-changers for bar chords. This might seem like a juggling act while practicing because it can be a lot to keep in mind while you're fretting a chord.

Don't worry, because it will all become effortless with time. It's just like riding a bicycle, a motorcycle, or driving a car; your brain ends up automating the whole thing.

Let's get started!

Your Thumb's Position is Paramount

Opposite to what most people think, the thumb is not the one doing the pressing effort for bar chords. Yes, many beginners make the same mistake when starting with bar chords and apply too much strength in a futile spot.

As a result, the effort is titanic and bar chords still have dead-sounding strings.

Furthermore, making too much effort with your thumb or fingertips might even make you play out-of-tune chords. Yes, when too much strength is applied you can either change a note's pitch or bend it. In both scenarios, your chord will sound awkward, to say the least.

So, the first thing you need to think about is that the muscle making all the needed pressure is the one that's between your thumb and your index. Yes, you don't need to press either with the fingertips or the thumb, the pressure needs to be in the middle.

But how do we transform our thumb's position to occupy the one we need? Well, we need to move it down to the middle of the fingerboard. Yes, your thumb should be behind the third and fourth strings.

That way, you won't use it to make the pressing effort and you won't be wasting energy on a move that won't get you closer to cleaner-sounding bar chords.

Let's take a look at what your thumb should look like:

The Index Finger Needs to Start Rolling

The title isn't just because I'm a die-hard Rolling Stones fan but because you need to roll the index finger literally to get better results.

I've seen this happen so many times that it is vital to address it in this book. To begin with, let's say that your index finger features different pressing surfaces. It has a fleshier, more irregular side, and a more even side that's closer to the bone.

So, the part you shouldn't use is the bottom, flat side, where the palm continues to turn into fingers. On the contrary, what you should do is use the side part of your finger that's harder and even

To press down with that side of the finger you have to roll it to the side.

Ideally, the part of the finger doing the pressing will be the side part while the thumb seats at the middle of the neck and you can make the pressure with the muscle between the index and the thumb.

This is what it looks like:

The Wrist, it's all in The Wrist

We could safely say that the position of your wrist is determined by the position of the fingers and the hand. Therefore, once you learn to lower your thumb and roll your index, your wrist will very much find its position without you doing anything with it.

Yet, that's not the whole picture; we have a couple of aces up our sleeves that can be game-changers for you.

To begin with, lower the wrist by accompanying the thumb and index movement. You'll notice that by lowering your thumb to the middle, your hand gains more strength.

Also, another great trick to elevate the strength levels in your fretting hand is using the arm or elbow on your picking hand to bring the guitar forward as you press it backward.

Wait, what? Forward? Backward? What a mess!

It sounds complicated, but it's very simple. If you use your picking hand to push the guitar toward your body as you play (maybe with the elbow or the arm), the neck of the guitar will tend to go forward, away from your body.

Thus, you'll be helping your index, thumb, and wrist to press down.

FAQs: Is it Common to Feel Wrist and Thumb Pain?

1.   Is it common to feel wrist pain?

Feeling pain in the wrist is very common when you're starting to play the guitar. This is simply because you're forcing your wrist to do things it has never done before. Thus, if you feel that your wrist is in pain after working your bar chords for a while, don't freak out; it's perfectly normal.

2.   What do I do about wrist pain?

Several solutions apply to wrist pain, especially when playing new chords. Let's go through the options to avoid it.

» Take short, quick rests to shake and stretch your hand while you're playing. Usually (at least for me) 1 minute of shaking and stretching the hand can do the magic and allow me to continue playing painlessly.

» Playing guitar is a hand workout. Therefore, like any other workout, it requires the hand to build muscle strength to perform better. So, in a nutshell, be patient and practice hard, your strength is coming.

» Drop the shoulder while you're trying to play bar chords. This is a very common mistake I've seen people make a lot while trying to master bar chords: they just concentrate so much on the wrist and thumb that they stiffen the shoulder and, as a result, get a rigid wrist. On the other hand, try loosening both shoulders and, as the shoulder drops, you'll realize the wrist movement will be effortless.

3.　Why does my thumb hurt?

Let me start this FAQ about your thumb with a newsflash: you don't need to make pressure on the strings with your thumb. Yes, if your thumb hurts, chances are you're using it to make more pressure and press on the strings harder. That is a big mistake because you're pushing too hard on a finger that's not going to help you play cleaner chords. So, your thumb hurts because you're pushing too hard with the wrong muscles. Always remember that the thumb is just an anchor for your fretting hand.

4.　How can I avoid thumb pain?

Now that you know why you have thumb pain, it's time to talk about how we avoid thumb pain while practicing bar chords. Let's go through the best three tips I can give you about it:

» The strength is in another muscle that doesn't belong to your thumb or fingers. Yes, the pressure to create perfect, clean chords (with or without a bar) comes from the muscle that's between your thumb and your index finger. Focusing your efforts on that muscle will alleviate thumb pain.

» Mind the thumb's height. When we use the thumb wrapped around the fingerboard, our hand's grip loses strength. On the other hand, when it's too low, we can't maneuver right or make it press hard enough. Therefore, the perfect position for the thumb is in the middle of the neck, right behind the middle strings (3rd and 4th).

» Don't press harder, have the guitar make all that effort for you. Yes, to make a clean-sounding bar chord on the guitar, you need to press several notes down together. You can make that pressure by pushing the guitar up into the hand while keeping it firm. Let's try this, form the B major chord above and take your thumb away from the guitar. With your picking hand, push the guitar's body toward you and the neck into the hand. You'll see that the thumb was less necessary than you thought.

Conclusion

Have you seen the movie Matrix? In the scene when Morpheus fights Neo, Laurence Fishburne tells Keanu Reeves, "Do you think me being faster or stronger has anything to do with my muscles in this place?" Well, the same rule applies to playing bar chords: it's not about how strong you are but about how to place your hands to make it as effortless as possible.

Thus, if you follow the techniques and tips that I shared with you in this first chapter, you'll very likely go through the physical side of playing bar chords easier and with less effort.

Remember, once you train your brain to use the right muscles in the right position, you too will be able to conquer any guitar-related obstacle coming your way.

CHAPTER 2

The B Major Chord in Action

Hey there! You made it through chapter 1 safe and sound; congratulations!

Welcome to chapter 2. This chapter is all about putting what you've just learned into action and getting a new concept called "chord progression" which I'll explain in a bit. But that's not all, because we're going to add two different strumming patterns per progression so you can practice with the picking hand as well.

This chapter will take us approximately 2 days to complete; we'll go through some diagrams, exercises, and of course, have a lot of fun.

Guitar, pen, paper, and a metronome are all you need to get started.

Let's do this!

DAY 3

The B Major Chord in its Natural Habitat

If we were to make an analogy and transform chords into animals, we could say that chords are, by design, social creatures. Yes, it is very strange to come across a lonely chord in modern music; we mostly hear them with other chords in the shape of songs.

Well, since it's their natural habitat, primary function, and most-common scenario, that's exactly how we're going to study them: surrounded by their friends.

Let me introduce the concept of chord progression to you. We'll see it in-depth later on in the book, but let's get started with three keys about them:

» Chord Progressions are made of a succession of chords. The order in which they are played and the quality of each of those chords affects the resulting song or musical piece as a whole.

» Chord progressions tell a story that's parallel to the one being told by the lyrics; chords convey emotions. Hence, by blending different chords, you can take the listener to a specific mood, scenario, and feel.

» Chord progressions aren't arbitrary; they are usually studied formulas that represent a musical style, a time and age, and an intention.

Those are three important keys about chord progressions but the true outcome of this chapter is to help you move from a bar chord to an open chord and vice versa. Furthermore, you'll learn these chord changes in the context of a chord progression, thus, you'll be acquiring two skills simultaneously.

Strumming Patterns, Your Picking Hand's Duty

I started this chapter by saying that we were going to learn some cool strumming patterns. You probably smiled when you saw the line but do you know what strumming patterns are?

Furthermore, do you know why they are so important?

Well, a strumming pattern can start a musical revolution.

Yes, it happened many times in the past with styles such as Rhythm & Blues, Rock and Roll, Disco, Pop, Punk, Metal, and many, many others.

We're not going to go so far in this book but we're going to educate the picking hand to do what we want instead of using a standard strumming pattern to play all songs.

That is what we call the "napping in the park" effect. It is the guitar player holding the acoustic guitar going from classic to classic and strumming everything the same. The sound becomes monotonous, and suddenly, you fall asleep and wake up to the thunderous roar of all your friends singing Wonderwall out loud.

But stories apart, it is very important that you practice these exercises with the right strumming pattern and a metronome to get the most out of this lesson.

Exercise 1

This is a very simple chord progression and a movement you have already practiced. What's new for this exercise is that you'll have to play these two chords while creating a particular strumming pattern with your picking hand.

My recommendation is that you start practicing slowly and then increase the tempo until you feel comfortable with it.

The chords we'll be using are A major and B major, the diagrams are a few pages back.

Picking Hand

This exercise offers you two very simple strumming patterns. When you encounter the V sign, it means a downward strum, and when you see a ∧ sign, it means an upward strum. Beware of the different time figures we have: quarter notes and eighth notes mixed; make sure you play twice on the third beat.

Try the strumming pattern over muted strings, then over a chord, and finally mixing it all up.

PRO TIP

Your metronome is paramount to becoming a better musician. Yes, all the time-bound exercises inside this book should be done with a metronome. A mind-blowing guitar player who can play at the speed of light is just another amateur musician until he or she can master time.

Become a master of your tempo practicing every exercise with a metronome. By the end of the book, you'll have acquired yet another paramount skill.

Exercise 2

We're introducing a new player to the game, a chord that I'm sure you're very familiar with: E major. Yes, that'll be our first chord to open the progression, then we move over to A, then the almighty B major, and finish with another

A major.

This simple chord progression will help you maneuver between two different chord shapes. Indeed, A and B major can be formed with a simple horizontal movement but to form an E major you have to change the entire hand's position.

Try that slowly at first and speed up as you see fit.

Picking Hand

The strumming patterns in this exercise combine up and down strokes in quarter notes only, so it's simpler to strum.

For the first version, you have mostly down strokes. Make sure you land on time on every stroke.

For the second exercise, what you have is two up and two down strokes so you can practice both movements.

Just like in the previous exercise, move from muted strings to chord progression slowly.

You'll find the track to hear what it sounds like in our bonus material.

PRO TIP

A very good skill to add to the collection is what I call "movement economy". What is this new concept I'm bringing to the table? Well, it's the idea that we can find a way to move from one shape to the next minimizing the effort.

Try this, put the A major shape on the strings and think of the easiest way to move your fingers and make an E major. Do you have to move them all? Can you move any of them in a block? Practice that with every chord change, and you'll improve your skills enormously.

DAY 4

Exercise 3

Don't freak out about how long this exercise looks, because it's just the same length as the ones you've played so far but played in eighth notes.

In this case, we have another very simple chord progression that involves 3 open chords and a B major. Make sure you practice the horizontal move from A to B and change your fretting hand to accommodate that E.

Picking Hand

If you pay close attention, you'll realize both strumming patterns are the same but inverted. Yes, the idea is that you realize that starting your strumming pattern by going up or down makes the world of difference. Have fun.

Exercise 3.1

Exercise 3.2

Exercise 4

This exercise is a summary of everything we've seen so far and introduces a new player you must already be familiar with: D major.

Perhaps, the main challenge this exercise proposes is that it mixes figures a lot. Also, it offers a two-chords-in-one-bar section so you can practice a quick horizontal movement from B to A.

Finally, pay special attention to the last half note, because it is your grand finale and you need to land on it on time and let it ring (while the screaming fans bring down the building!).

Exercise 4.1

Exercise 4.2

Picking Hand

The first version of this exercise offers you the possibility of playing a build-up sequence using down-strokes only with eighth notes (4 in a row). Then, you arrive at another section with down and up strokes until the grand finale.

On the second exercise, you start with a mix of quarter-and-eighth notes and take a deep breath with the half note to launch into a frantic down-stroke-fueled ramp-up through 10 consecutive notes (2 quarter and 8-eighth notes).

Finally, you reach the last E major and give your fans two final strums. If you make silence and close your eyes, you can hear them clapping and singing your name.

FAQ – I Can Hold the Shape, but Sounding Muted

The first approach to bar chords is usually quite frustrating. The feeling is that of a juggler trying to apply every single piece of information you've learned to the shape you're forming with your hands.

For starters, you need to roll the index finger. Following, stop using your thumb or other fingers to press down on the strings and start using your elbow to push your guitar into your hands.

Next, you need to remember to use the muscle between the thumb and the index to press strings down. Speaking of which, you need to lower the thumb down to the middle of the neck (between the 3rd and 4th strings).

Finally, you need to learn the shape and form it properly on the fretboard.

All of this might be a lot and your mind might not be able (yet) to follow all these indications at once.

Worry not, by the time you finish the book, we will transform that experience into an automatized order that your brain can interpret and follow effortlessly.

What I'm trying to say is that, if you find it very hard to make your B major ring like an open chord, hold the shape on the neck and do your best. Little by little, the individual strings of your chord will sound loud and proud.

Be patient, practice hard, and you'll be playing bar chords perfectly in a matter of days.

CHAPTER 3

The Almighty F Major Chord

After playing the B major chord on the 5th string, it is time to move up and start forming chords with the root or tonic on the 6th string.

Yes, this is what you can call graduating from 5th-string bar chords and going up one level to a harder scenario. I'm not going to lie to you, making a bar chord with 6 strings is a tad harder than doing it with 5 strings.

That being said, the bar chords you're about to learn, with a root on the 6th string are among the most used bar chords in music history. You'll be playing those as long as you play guitar.

We'll work on this chapter for three days. During that time, we'll go through a plethora of tips, diagrams, and detailed instructions so you can conquer this new skill once and for all.

Are you ready to take it to the next level?

Let's do this!

DAY 5

Let's Get Started with an E Major Chord

Just like we built the B major chord starting from our A major chord, we're going to use the E major chord to form our almighty F major. As you might know already, the open 6th string is the tonic or root note of our E major. Hence, since F is one semitone away from E, you only need to move the same shape one fret toward the bridge and add the F on the 6th string first fret to transform the E major into an F major.

Yet, this time we'll do it a little differently because instead of putting together an F chord, we'll create an A major chord on the fifth fret.

Wait, what?! Isn't this chapter called F major? How do I create an A major on the fifth fret?

Yes, it is; and yes, we're getting there. We're going to go through several versions and chords before arriving at our F major chord.

Be patient and follow these instructions, believe me, by the time you make it to the F major, it will be easier to play.

These are the reasons why we chose A major instead of F major to start practicing:

» Fret spacing – By moving the bar chord shape to the fifth fret, the spacing between the frets becomes friendlier to form a bar chord.

» You get more room for the index finger – The nut in your guitar is very close to your first fret. This leaves less room for the finger you want to use for the bar chord. Also, strings are harder to fret when you're so close to the nut. Hence, moving the structure to the 5th fret makes it easier.

Let's take a look at the shapes we're using before we go deep into how to play the new 6-string bar chord.

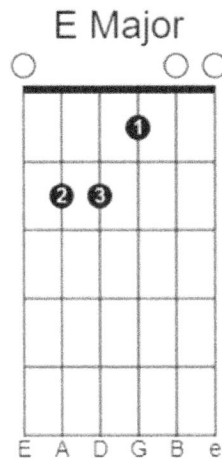

Now, instead of moving that same shape toward the fifth fret, I'm going to teach you a smaller version of the bar chord that you can use all over the fretboard too. You might think of it as a shortcut to use while you're learning.

Moreover, it shares the same principle bar chords do, and, as long as you can keep the same shape and move it, you can create a different chord named after the tonic or root note. Speaking of which, instead of looking for the root note on the 6th string you need to look for it on the 1st string (in standard tuning, notes repeat in these strings).

So, let's see what our A major looks (and sounds) like with this first approach:

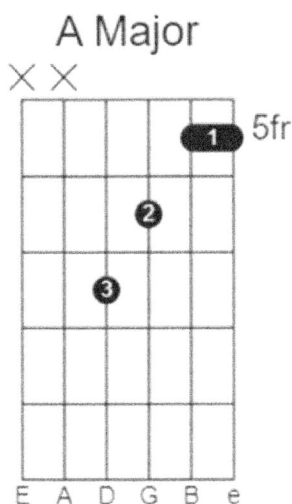

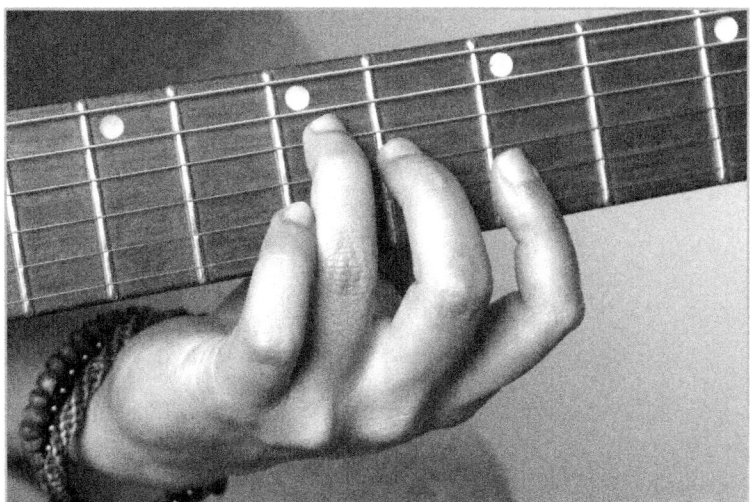

Bear in mind that you don't have to strum the top two strings because the notes they generate aren't part of the chord. Therefore, you should only play strings 4, 3, 2, and 1.

Pay close attention to the way your strings sound when you fret this chord; you should be able to hear them loud and clear.

Let's turn that into a full bar chord.

For this, we need to use our index finger to fret all the strings from one to six.

Plus, do you notice any difference between the E major chord and this A major chord? Yes, we're lacking our 5th string finger. Therefore, we're going to add it to play a proper A major chord with its bar on the fifth fret.

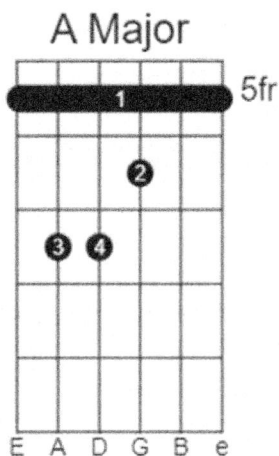

PRO TIP

Use your picking hand to play each of the notes individually and check that you have no dead or muted strings. If you do, fix that before moving on to the next string and finger. Believe me, although it is kind of annoying going string by string, it is the only effective way to spot and fix any issues with your bar chord. I call this the string-by-string technique.

DAY 6

Forming your First F Major Bar Chord

Now that you've fully mastered the A major chord, let's tackle the F chord.

So, to begin with we'll create the first shape involving strings 1 to 4 with the small bar on the first two strings.

Let's see what that looks like:

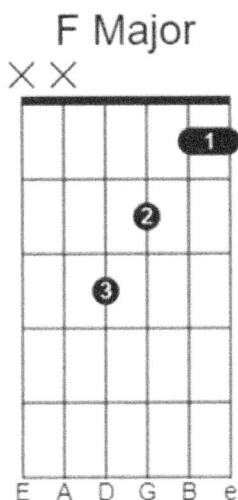

Was it harder than doing this at the 5th fret? Well, that's exactly why we started on the 5th fret and not on the 1st.

Use the string-by-string technique and make sure you're fretting all the strings properly and that the chord sounds clear.

Are you ready?

The time has come.

Let's play your first F major bar chord occupying all strings on your guitar. Remember that your index finger should focus its pressure on strings 1, 2, and 6. The rest of the strings are covered by the other fingers.

Without further ado, here's your F Major chord:

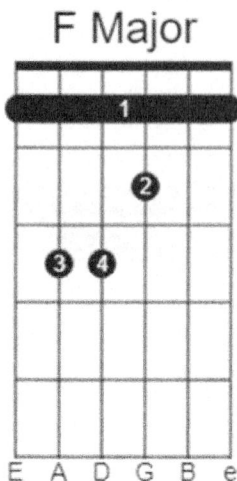

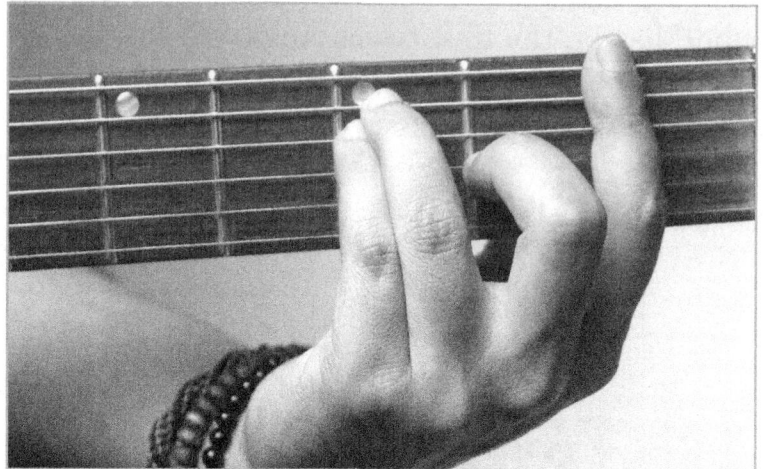

F Major

Having Problems with That Pinky Finger? Try This!

Sometimes, putting together a 4-finger chord is more complicated than assembling a 3-finger chord.

This section has everything to do with me and my musical journey.

This is because, when I was learning to play the guitar, I had to come up with a technique and a series of chords I could play without using the pinky. It took me a long while to tame that finger down, and during that time, I was playing dominant 7th chords instead of major chords.

Don't get me wrong, dominant 7th chords by no means replace major chords. They sound utterly different and fulfill a different role in music theory. That being said, the shape they have when on the fretboard isn't very different and is great for practicing.

Here's the A7 bar chord for you to practice an easy 3-finger bar chord.

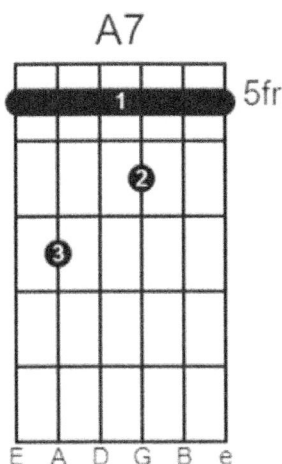

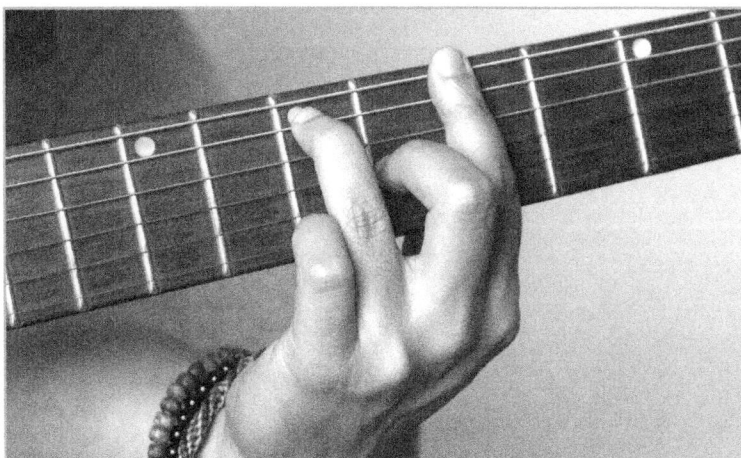

Things to keep in mind

Playing a bar chord that sounds perfectly well is something that takes time and effort. Yes, after practicing a lot your brain will just need to receive an order like "F# Major" to form the bar chord on the second fret sixth string.

These are the things you have to practice specifically to reach that glorious moment.

Yes, by practicing these techniques, you'll be taking shortcuts to get closer to playing bar chords whenever and wherever you need to.

Thumb

Your thumb is paramount to putting together a proper bar chord. This is especially true for chords that occupy all 6 strings of the guitar.

A very common mistake in this sense is placing your thumb parallel to the floor. This is wrong because when your thumb is in that position, you can't use it to make the pressure you need.

Instead, your thumb should be perpendicular to the floor, at the middle of the neck behind the bar chord, occupying the space behind strings 3 and 4.

Bad thumb position

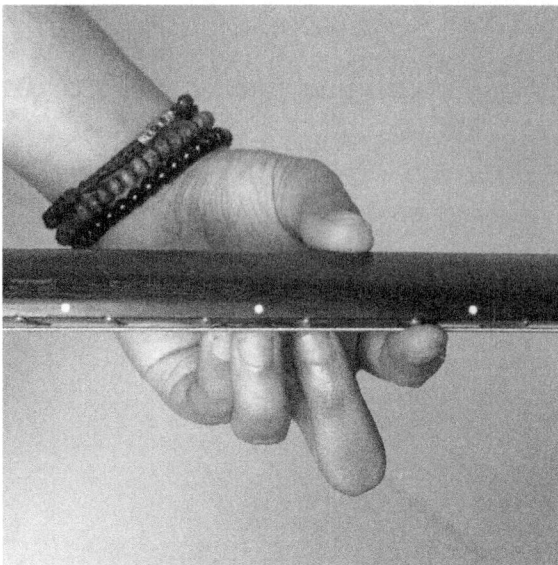

Good position angle 1

Good position angle 2

Wrist

The wrist is another paramount aspect to master when trying to play bar chords. Indeed, the position of the wrist can be a game-breaker since it also affects the position of the thumb.

So, what should we do with our wrist when trying to play the F major bar chord? Well, all our efforts should be focused on the wrist being down and out. Yes, the moment you move your thumb as described above, you'll realize the wrist tends to go lower and out; that's the correct position for it.

Fingers

The position of the thumb and the wrist will define the position of your fingers as well.

As you know, fingers are not the same in every section of their surface. On the contrary, we need to find the most suitable, harder, and even parts of our fingers to make pressure on the strings.

Let's see two characteristics our finger position should have:

> » Your finger presses better with its side rather than the middle. This goes for the index finger (we already talked about rolling it) but also for the rest of the fingers. Yes, you should use the top of your fingertips and place your fingers very close to the fret; therefore it's very likely you press with the top side of your fingertips.

» Do not let your fingers bend backward. This is a symptom of you pressing too hard with the wrong muscles. If you feel like your fingers are bent backward or the tips get extremely white, then you have to revise what you're pressing with. Try and focus all the pressing effort on the elbow-on-the-body technique and on the muscle between the thumb and index.

Don't let the fingers bend backwards

Simple Fretboard Hack

Finally, before we wrap this chapter up, let me give you a piece of advice that saved me more times than I can remember.

We said at the beginning that the E major chord has its root note on the open 6th string. Therefore, if we move our index finger over that string, we can form any major chord we need by simply moving the same shape around, and using a new root note.

Thus, if you know all the notes on the 6th and 5th strings by heart, you'll know where to find the bar chords you need.

These are all the notes for these two strings. Remember, major chords with the root note on the 6th string are based on E major and major chords with the root on the 5th string are based on A major.

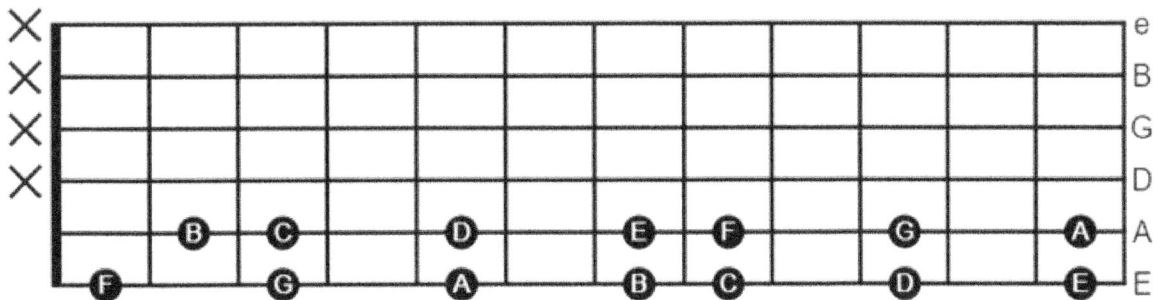

CHAPTER 4

F Major in Action

Just like it happened with our B major chord, we won't find an F major in the wild on its own. You already know this; chords like to go around in packs causing mayhem in the shape of songs.

Therefore, seeing them interact with other chords is the perfect way to get to know more about them. Furthermore, in this chapter, we're not only going to practice F major a lot, but you will also get to learn three new strumming patterns, practice how to go from open chord to bar chord and back, and also a few chord progressions.

This chapter will take us 2 days to complete, and, during that time, you're going to play a lot.

Go get your favorite guitar and get ready to learn the F major in its favorite habitat.

Let's do this!

DAY 7

Finding an F Major in its Natural Habitat

Let's get started by saying that the natural habitat for a chord is a composition. Yes, chords belong with the gang, with other chords.

Moreover, it is this interrelation between different textures, flavors, tones, and emotions that make music an integral part of our lives. Yes, chords have a lot to do with haunting your senses; they tell a story, convey emotions, and take you on a journey.

I've prepared six exercises so you can practice your chord changes, feel the power of the F major, and have some fun while learning this new skill.

Oh, one more thing, you can use a capo and transform every F major into an A major by placing it on the fourth fret (leaving the fifth fret empty for that big index of yours). This will make it easier to play the bar chord. Then, you can just add the open chords in the same position and they will work perfectly, trust me.

Do you have your guitar ready? If not, go get it and let's go straight into exercise 1.

Exercise 1

Exercise 1 is a pretty straightforward chord progression that starts with the utterly known C major and then goes to a slash chord (G/B) for which you'll see the diagram just below. After the slash chord you go to a minor chord that dyes everything blue and the big finish comes from the strong statement made by your F major.

What is a Slash Chord?

Slash chords are very common in modern music. There's absolutely no hidden trick about them, it's just a chord with a different lowest note. For example, if we want to play C but change the lowest now for G to add bottom-end, we can just play it over the C on the sixth string third fret.

In this case, this slash chord is a G (the letter on the left is the chord) with a B as the lowest note.

Here are both diagrams.

You'll find the track to hear what it sounds like in our bonus material.

Picking Hand

For exercises 1 and 2, the picking pattern is completely straightforward. The only thing you have to make sure of is to land on the first beat of the bar with a downstroke and then use up and down alternatively.

Exercise 2

The chord progression for exercise 2 is a little more complex-sounding since it involves a seventh chord. So, you go from the C major chord to the seventh chord and then move on to finish the exercise with the same minor + major formula.

The picking pattern is the same as in exercise 1.

Exercise 3

For exercise 3 I decided to move the F major from the last and strong statement of the song to a chord that could bring us to an ending. Again, you start on the almighty C major chord, move to A minor, and then the tandem of the two major chords make this progression end on a high note.

Picking Hand

The picking hand in this exercise is a tad more complex because it involves a mixture of eight and quarter notes. To play it properly, use a metronome, and make sure you land on the first beat with a down stroke for every chord. Also, bear in mind that the upward movement is only on the eighth note.

DAY 8

Exercise 4

For exercise 4, we brought everything up a notch. Moreover, starting the chord progression with a strong F major and adding two minor and two seventh chords give this exercise different colors and textures. On top of that, you have two bars that share chords, the first and third.

Yes, I know, we went "everything to eleven, please".

So, practice quick chord changes in bars 1 and 3, and pay close attention to the picking pattern, especially in bars 2 and 4. As you might have noticed, it is the same as in exercise 3.

Exercise 5

This chord progression in exercise 5 has the particularity that it starts and ends with an F major chord. These are strong opening and closing statements.

Moreover, the presence of seventh chords (A7 and E7), as well as the D minor in the middle make this progression another heavily textured piece. Make the most out of these chord changes by playing them time and time again until you can grasp the uniqueness of those tones.

Picking Hand

The picking pattern in this exercise changed if you compare it with the previous two. That being said, the idea is very similar with the difference that you have four eighth notes together in the middle with two quarter notes to begin and finish. This increases the intensity of each bar whether it is a two-chord bar or a single-chord bar. Pay attention to how the ending in a quarter note with an F major releases tension.

Exercise 6

For this final exercise, we changed the order around and did a move that I'll explain more about when I get to the upcoming FAQ. Yes, you have to move between two very close chords: Am and A7. These chords only differ by the A in the third string second fret, and the C in the second string first fret, thus, you can use them to practice economy in movement.

Finally, the order between E7 and G is different, but the grandiloquent ending with the F major is still there.

FAQ: I Can Play the Bar Chord, But Am Not Able to Switch between Chords

I decided to add this FAQ at the end of this chapter because I think it's paramount to address this issue many students of mine have had in the past two decades.

Does the title ring a bell? Are you in the same situation?

Well, if you are, then it's good news!

How so? Well, very simply, it means you are having what we call "level 2 problems". These are problems that are not related to step 1 which is forming and playing the bar chord but to step 2, making that bar chord just another chord in the sequence.

What can you do to make this transition easier?

What has always worked for me is the "progressive chord change technique". You need to follow only three simple steps and it will be a leap forward in your quest to master bar chords.

Let's go through the steps:

1. The first step is to study the chords you're about to play. To do this successfully, what you need to do is to form those chords on the fretboard without playing them. Pay close attention to the movement between one chord and the next.

2. The second step is to look for common notes and minimum movement options. For example, moving from Am to C is to move one finger. Other examples we've seen in this book are from E to F and from A to B. Look for the common notes and the minimum movement tackling one chord change at a time.

3. The final step is to repeat step number 1 but with the newly-acquired chord change strategy. Make sure you don't incorporate the right hand just yet and focus only on the movements of the fretting hand. Once it feels good, try playing the sequence with a metronome.

This technique works for any kind of chord change you're aiming for and you can utilize it for the rest of your career. I know; you're welcome.

CHAPTER 5

Minor Chords

Major chords are everyone's favorites for being upbeat and fun. Moreover, they are better-known and more widely used than minor chords in pop music.

Yet, minor chords bring in the emotional side to music.

Yes, not every tune you hear requires you to twist and shout like a maniac. On the opposite, sometimes music's most delicate gems are hidden in those sad songs, ballads destined to be B-Sides of a 7" single.

Well, capturing the magic of minor chords isn't easy but you're going to learn two shapes in two days that will allow you to play any minor chord rooted on the fifth and sixth strings.

Go get your favorite six-stringer because we're in for a ride to the emotional side of bar chords.

DAY 9

Getting Started, the Almighty F Minor (Fm)

We've seen the F major bar chord shape derived from E major. Well, if I was to put together an F minor, what chord should I base it on? You got it, E minor.

But how do I transform a two-finger chord into a bar chord?

Well, just like we did with F major, we need to change the root note of the chord from E to F. Once we've done that, we have to transform that root note into a bar.

Let's see the diagrams so you can appreciate the transition better:

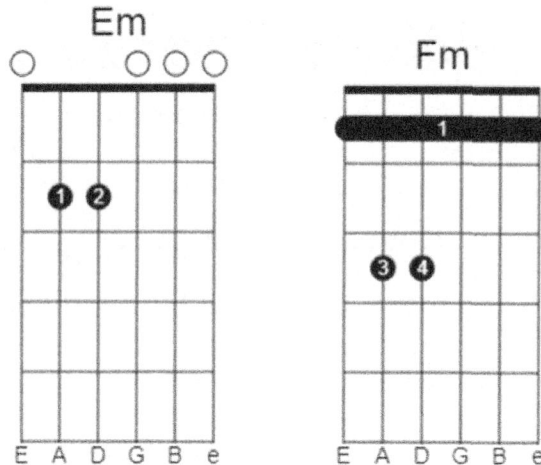

Furthermore, if we apply what we have just learned about the economy of movement to the change between F major and F minor, what we get is a single finger of difference: third string second fret.

So, if you want to turn your F major into F minor you only have to move one finger.

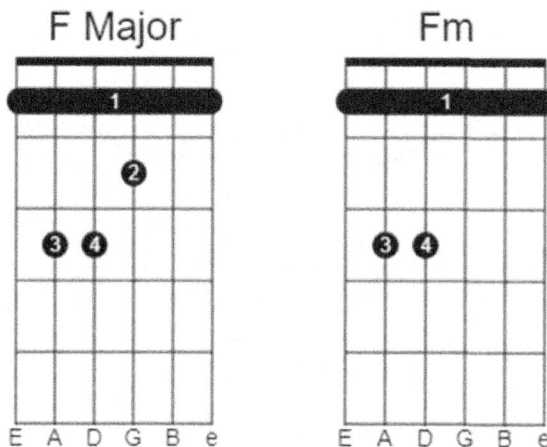

PRO TIP

With time I developed a way to play minor bar chords with the root on the sixth string. I called it the "stacked index". Yes, I should work on naming things for companies, I know, but I love guitar too much for that.

Dreams aside, back to my pro tip. This is a very simple technique that helps your index finger fret this chord. Yes, this help will come in the shape of a physical backup played by your middle finger.

How so? Well, you have to put your middle finger parallel to the index and press down with both fingers at the same time. This extra help will be a relief when you want to make fast changes and also for those difficult first three strings.

It looks like this:

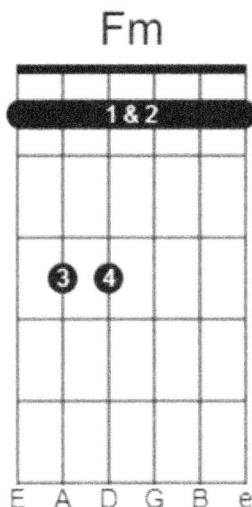

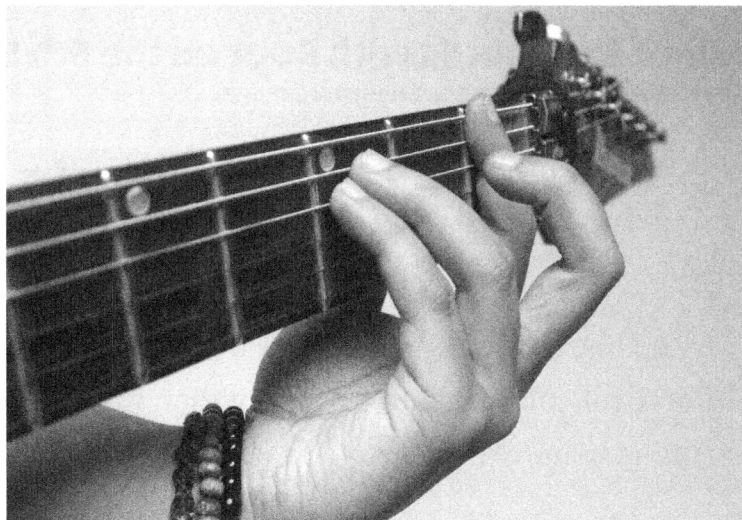

F minor angle 1

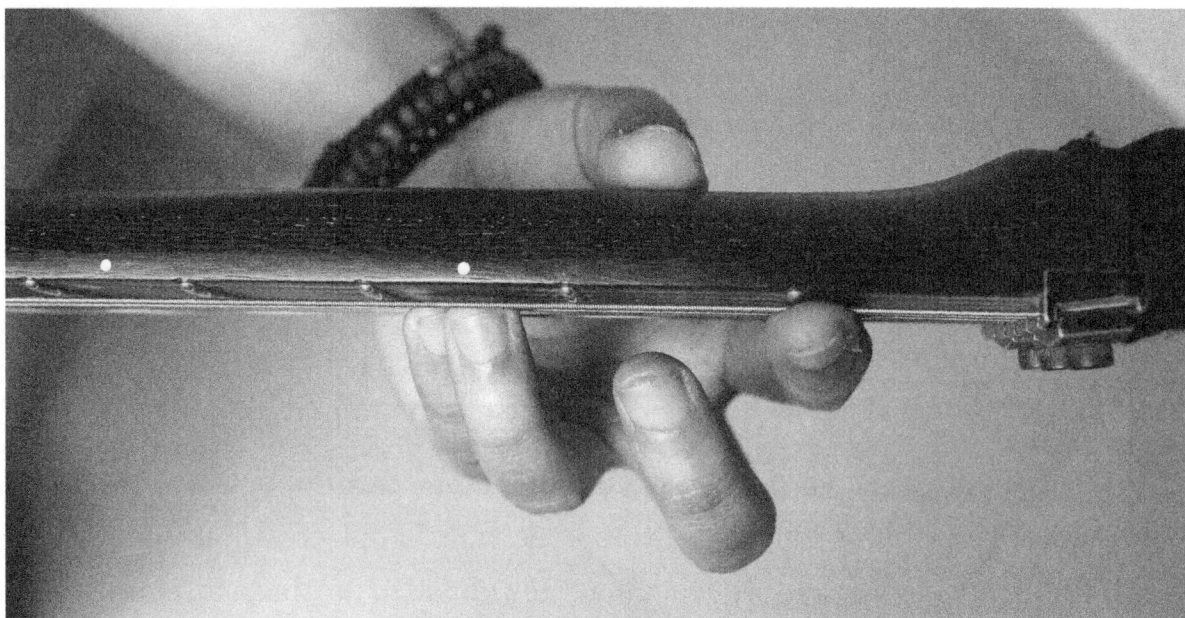

F Minor angle 2

DAY 10

Minor Bar Chords with Root on the 5th String: Cm

Not everything in the life of a guitar player is stacking fingers to cover six strings; on the contrary, other chords don't require that much effort from the player.

Yes, although there is a sound difference (that low 6th string makes a big difference), playing minor and major bar chords with the root on the 5th string is usually easier.

Back to the Cm, if we used A major to put together our B major chord, what do you think we'll use to create a C minor? Yes, you guessed it again, A minor!

Yet, A minor's root is the open 5th string. We need to turn that root into a C to play the C minor chord. Where is C on the 5th string? Yes, on the third fret (as long as your guitar is in standard tuning).

So, what we'll do is simply take a look at these chords and witness that magical transformation:

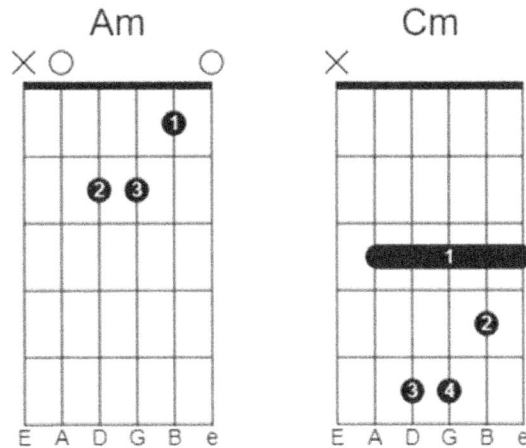

This shape, unadulterated, can give you all minor chords with a root on the 5th string. All you have to do is memorize the notes on that string and move the same shape throughout the neck.

Also, thinking about movement economy, the move from A major to A minor is simply transforming the C# to C (second string second and first frets). Well, here you have to do the same because the difference between major and minor bar chords with the root on the 5th fret is also one note.

Going from C major to C minor looks like this:

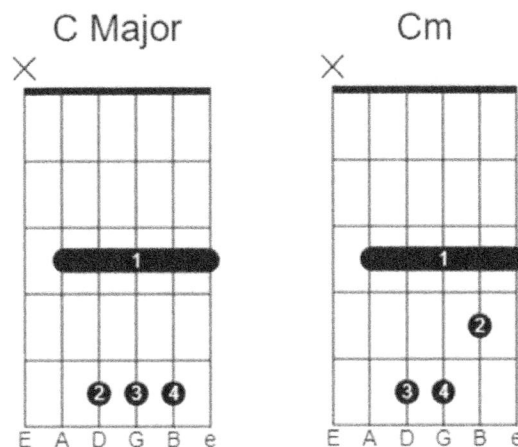

PRO TIP

Many players (me included) like to think that the shape of a minor bar chord with a root on the fifth string is the same as the one on a major bar chord with the root on the 6th string. Why is this important, you might ask? Well, simply because if you learn how to keep the form in place forming the new chord by moving one string up, you can go from major to minor and vice versa very easily.

For example, if you need to play Cm and G major, it's more convenient to play the major chord with a bar because you only have to move the same structure up or down.

It looks like this:

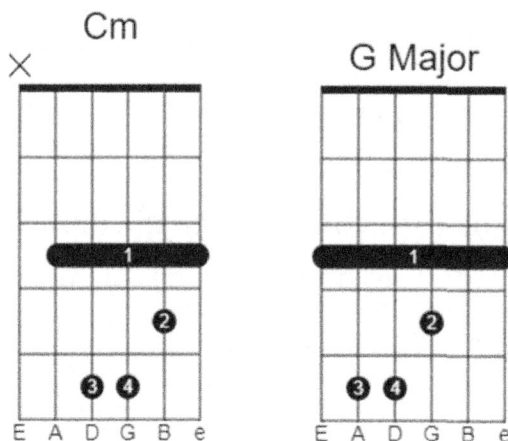

C minor angle 1   C minor angle 2

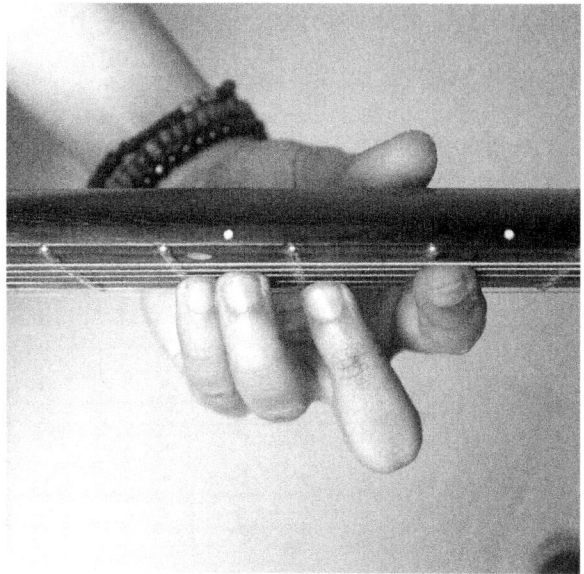

DAY 11

Minor Chord Shapes in Chord Progressions

As we've seen before, chords like hanging out with friends in songs. Songs are made of a combination of chords we called chord progressions.

The big difference between the previous and these chord progressions is that everything will be dyed of a different color with the minor chords.

Pay close attention, especially to the second progression that starts with a minor chord. You'll notice that it is a major difference unleashed by a detail.

Exercise 1

This is a great exercise to practice movement economy while mastering minor bar chords. Yes, for starters, you can go from C to Am by moving one finger, your ring finger from the fifth string third fret to the third string second fret.

Secondly, transforming your F major into the minor version only takes one finger, as we saw above.

Practice these moves before the exercise and they will help you get better results.

Exercise 2

This is a classic, four-chords-and-four-bars exercise that will help you work on minor and major bar chords. To begin with, the Cm and the Fm are bar chords in different strings which is useful to practice. Following that, you can just move your hand down and form the Bb major on the first fret. Finally, finish with the open G chord for the grand finale.

Flat & Sharp Chords

Just as a little reminder, let's talk a bit about flats (b) and sharps (#).

These phenomena are what musicians call "accidents". If you're familiar with the keyboard of a piano, the white keys are the natural notes and the black keys are the accidents. These are found one semi-tone away from the natural note.

In guitar, a semi-tone is one fret, and a whole tone is two frets.

Sharps go up half a tone and flats go down half a tone

So, from B to Bb you have to move one fret down (toward the nut). On the contrary, to go from F to G, you have to move two frets from the first to the third fret of the sixth string.

The only exceptions to this rule are the intervals E – F and B – C. These chords are separated by half a tone; therefore, E# and Fb don't exist just like B# or Cb.

For more information about this and a proper, detailed discussion, you can refer to chapter 8.

FAQ: Do I Need to Go to The Gym to Play Bar Chords?

This is a question I've had to answer more times than I would like. Yet, it is a trick question because playing bar chords IS going to the gym.

Yes, I know, the way you strengthen muscles is by using them. Unfortunately, nobody has invented the machine to use for the specific muscles you need for bar chords as you would your pectorals, biceps, or quadriceps.

Therefore, the only way that bar chords are getting easier to play is by playing them a lot.

Follow our exercises, they make playing bar chords fun.

I promise that, although you'll get better, you won't even notice you're going to the gym.

CHAPTER 6

Dominant Chords

We went from the upbeat happiness of major chords to the sweet and sad taste of minor chords. Now, we're taking everything a notch further by introducing a new set of chords that play a key role in modern music.

These are the dominant chords. These chords are built around the dominant note of the scale, and thus, carry the same dominant function the note does. This is to create tension and instability that can be resolved by playing the tonic.

Therefore, learning dominant chords is paramount to being a master of dynamics and making your audience feel an emotional rollercoaster as they're hearing your music.

Go get your guitar, because this audience-hooking lesson starts right now and there's a lot of playing to do.

~ DAY 12 ~

Dominant Seventh Bar Chords, Introducing B7

We already established what dominant chords are; their seventh iteration is an even more effective version of these pivotal chords.

Yes, seventh bar chords are great songwriting tools that will allow you to accentuate anything you need as a writer. Indeed, by generating that much tension, you can create a big contrast between song sections.

For example, bridges and seventh chords are a match made in heaven since they make a great tension-riser that can be the perfect entrance for a chorus that takes off on the root note.

As you know, root notes make amazing statements, especially for choruses.

So, let's put together our first seventh bar chord. If we used A major for B major and A minor for B minor, what shall we use for B7? Well done; yes, exactly A7.

To move from A major to A7 we need to remove the middle finger from the third string second fret.

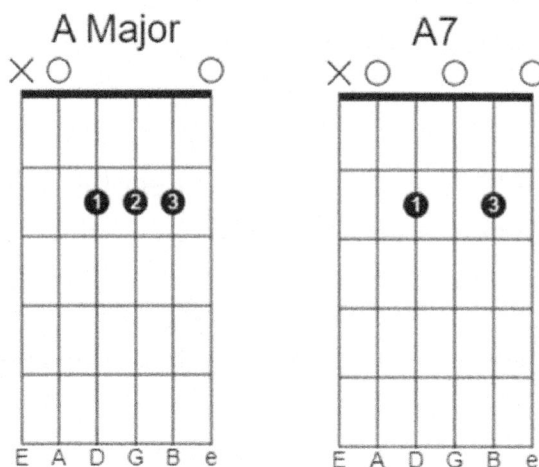

Moving from B major to B7 takes exactly the same effort, removing one finger.

Let's take a look at what that movement looks like:

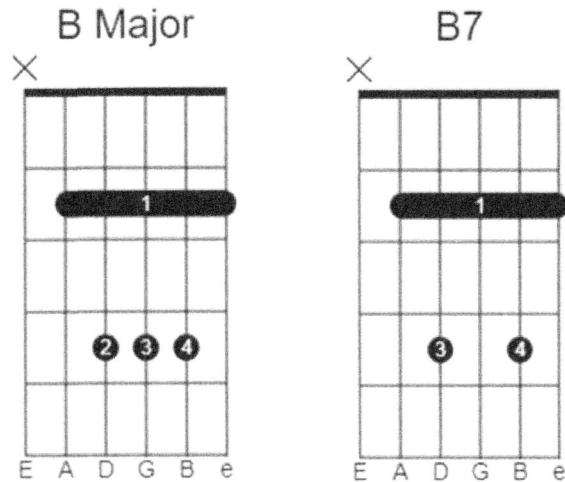

Just like you remove one finger to move from the open chord version of A to A7, you also remove one finger to go from B major to B7.

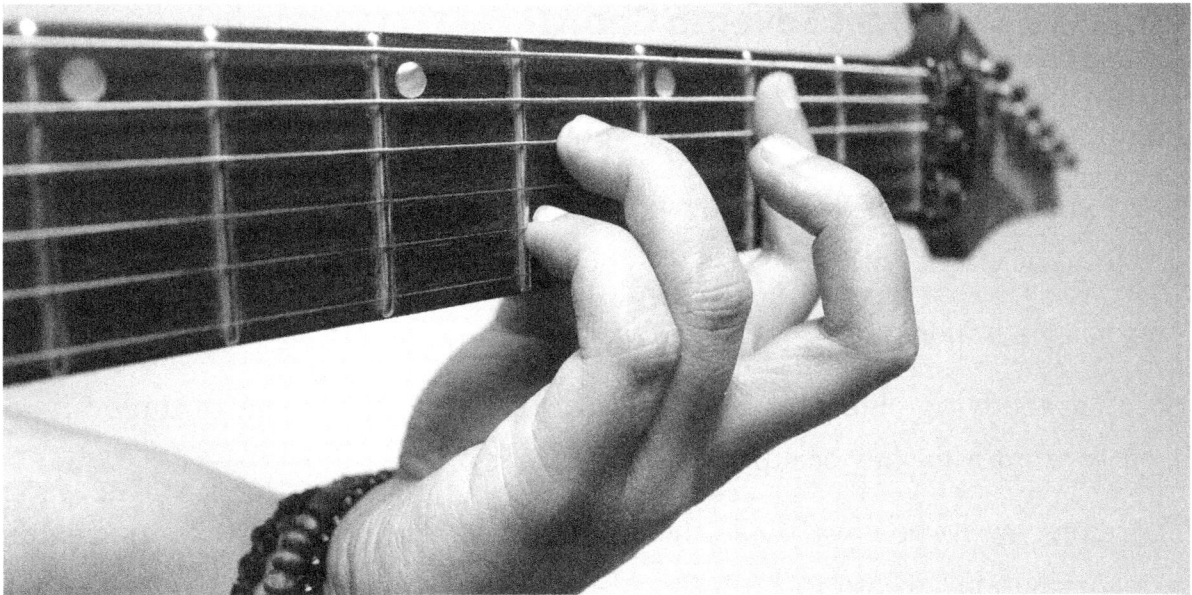

B7 angle 1

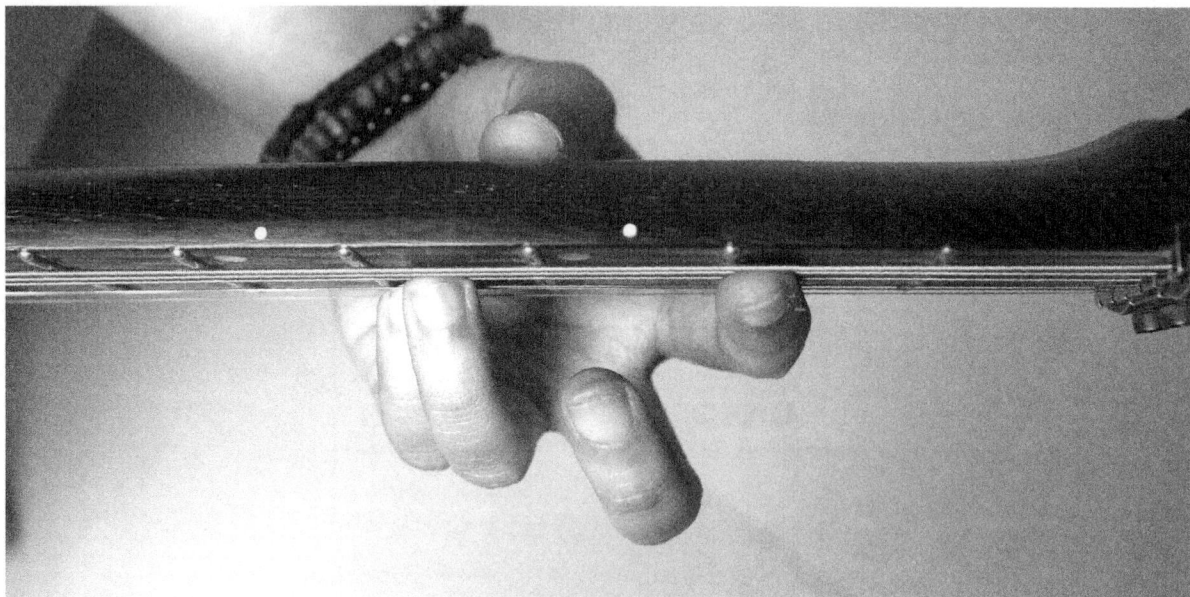

B7 angle 2

What is a Dominant Seventh Chord?

Dominant chords aren't new to you; you played them in chapter 5.

Now, we're going to go in a little deeper into the explanation of the function of a dominant chord within a series of chords or chord progression.

Why is this important?

Because studying chords in their natural habitat allows you to understand exactly what role they occupy in compositions.

Therefore, we'll see how to use the dominant seventh chords with its friends in a common progression.

To begin with, let's define a dominant chord: a dominant chord is the fifth degree of the scale. As we said before, its primary function is to generate tension that can be redeemed by playing the tonic.

A dominant seventh chord is a dominant chord on steroids.

For example, if we take the key of C to explain it, we can say that the dominant chord (V degree on the scale) is G.

Therefore, if we play G7, it will beg us to go back to C. This is because of the extra note that turns the dominant into a dominant seventh and gives it the needed urge to resolve.

C Major Scale						
I	II	III	IV	V	VI	VII
C	Dm	Em	F	G	Am	B Diminished

Let's do it as a test; try playing these chords first with the G major.

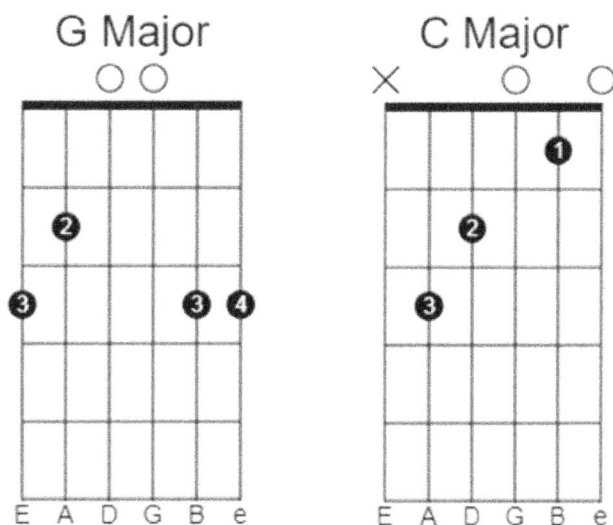

Now try it again but using the G7.

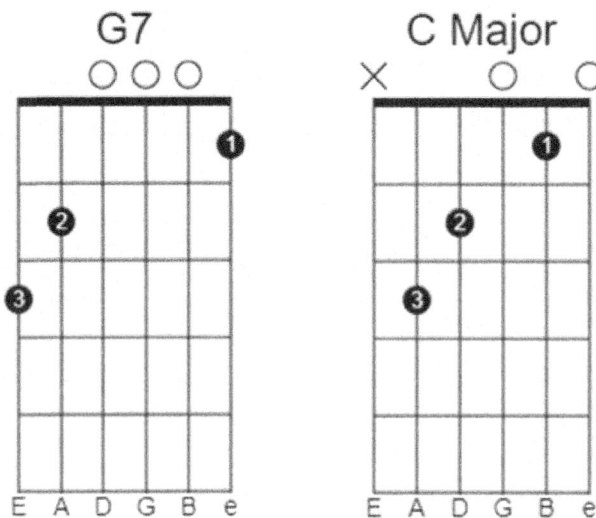

Can you feel the difference in urgency? Well, that's exactly what dominant seventh chords are all about.

Where to use a Dominant Seventh Chord?

Dominant seventh chords are great as part of a chorus, as a bridge, or in any other context where tension needs to be generated and released.

Although it used to be the rule of thumb to use seventh chords as a pivotal chord to go to the root, modern music has embraced the IV and the VI degree as possible resolutions too.

Of course, if you choose to go from the dominant to either of those, you'll find a different path for your story.

Let's pour this into an example. For that, let's use the scale of E major that has B as a dominant.

E Major Scale						
I	II	III	IV	V	VI	VII
E	F#m	G#m	A	B	C#m	D#°

Let's do the same exercise as before going from dominant IV (A), VI (C#m), and root or I (E), so you can hear and feel the difference.

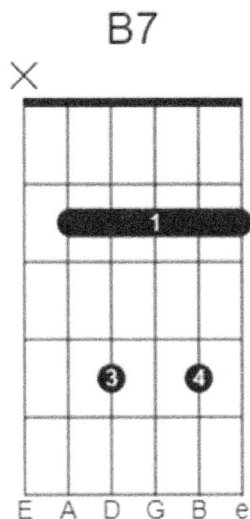

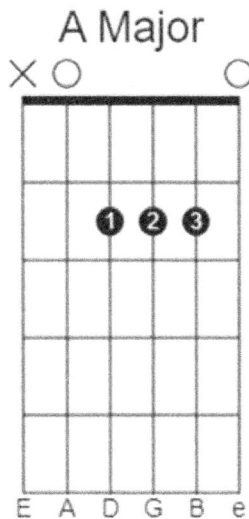

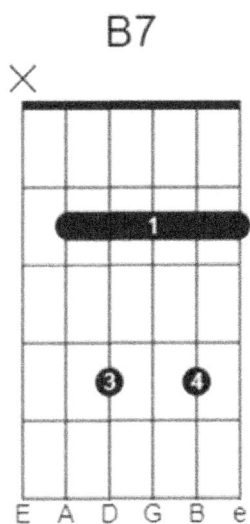

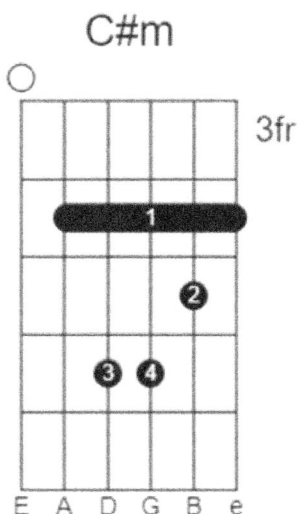

B7

A Major

B7

C#m

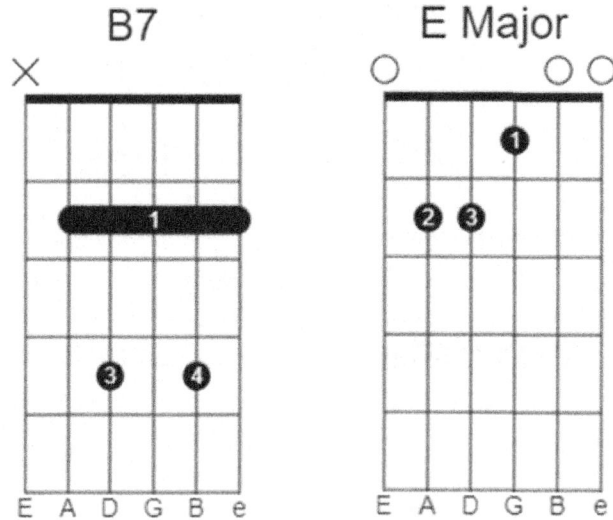

That was just a sneak peek at the power of the dominant seventh chords unleashed.

Let's see what they are capable of in these three chord progressions:

DAY 13

Exercise 1

Exercise 1 is great to continue practicing the economy of movement as you can go from B7 to Bm by making a simple finger swap. Yes, you have to move the pinky up one string and add the middle finger on the second string third fret to form the Bm chord.

Finally, the dual minor chords at the end leave the progression on a palatable sad note.

Exercise 2

For exercise 2, the idea is to see what happens with seventh dominant chords in a major-chord context. When played this way, this dominant seventh chord works only as a passing chord creating tension and then resolving one semitone above.

Exercise 3

Starting a chord progression with a minor chord sets the mood for what's coming next and this exercise is a great example of it. Also, the economy of movement is at its peak; we chose to play the Dm chord as a bar since you can move the same, unadulterated shape, and use it to play your G major on the sixth string.

DAY 14

Dominant Seventh Bar Chords, Introducing the Almighty F7

We saw how to put together a dominant seventh bar chord with the root or tonic on the fifth string. Now, what happens if we want to play a dominant seventh bar chord with root on the sixth string?

Yes, we have to change the shape. Instead of forming our F7 based on the A7, we're going to base it on the E7.

Let's see what that looks like in diagrams.

Just like it happened before, by moving the E7 one semi-tone up, what you get is an F7 chord.

Moreover, you can use the same shape to play any dominant seventh bar chord anywhere you want on the fretboard. Furthermore, you can always refer to the "Simple Fretboard Hack" in chapter 3 to memorize the notes and chords.

The Almighty F7 in a Chord Progression

The F7, and any other dominant seventh chord, can be a game-changer when used correctly. Moreover, we're going to experiment a little with using a seventh chord to end a chord progression and also we'll see what happens when we use more than one dominant seventh chord in a progression.

We have only two more exercises to finish this first part of the book, so get your six-stringer and let's practice these chords!

Oh, before I forget, these exercises, don't offer you a strumming pattern. You can use your favorite one.

Exercise 1

This first exercise is very simple and only includes three chords you already know. An important thing to bear in mind is that you can alternatively use C major as an open chord or as a bar chord simply lowering the index finger straight from the Gm and adding the middle finger.

Finally, the seventh chord works as a bridge to whatever comes next.

Exercise 2

Exercise one is very simple and this one requires a little more concentration.

The sequence starts with an F7 and then moves to a D7 as an open chord. This movement requires you to remove the bar and play only the four bottom strings. Bear this in mind as you're strumming.

Finally, the move from Gm to C7 is perfect to work on movement economy, since you can move almost the entire same shape one string up and down to form C7 from Gm.

Again, ending the composition on a C7 leaves the door open for adding another section.

FAQ How do I get rid of fatigue?

Hand fatigue seems to be the number-one enemy of bar-chord players.

Yes, I know many fellow guitarists, who can play at the speed of light, do sweep-picking, tapping, and know a million scales but can't play more than one song with bar chords.

Why do you think this happens? Well, the theoretical explanation is that you use two different muscles for these tasks. Yes, the slow-twitch muscles in our bodies use the energy slowly and evenly for longer periods and are prepared for endurance. On the other hand, the fast-twitch muscles use up a lot of energy really fast, and thus, feel fatigued much sooner.

Using fast-twitch muscles to play bar chords is, therefore, a recipe for disaster.

But why is this important?

Well, it was an introduction to say that you're on the right path but you have to work on the specific muscles required by bar chords until they become strong enough. Indeed, even if you have been playing for a while and can play scales at the speed of light, you need to build strength and endurance in the right muscles.

If time doesn't cure your hand fatigue, try these three tips:

» **Check your technique** – Technique is everything. If you have a faulty bar chord technique, you might be using up all your strength and not getting clear results. If that's the case, go back to the first chapters of this book and relearn the thumb position before trying again.

» **Don't press more than you have to** – This is another major problem for many players: pressing too much. Let me tell you that the strength you need to press strings and play a clean and beautiful bar chord doesn't come from your fingers. Instead, try and use the elbow-on-the-body technique to reduce the pressure needed from the hand.

» **Stretch before playing** – Just like athletes stretch their muscles before engaging in the activity they perform, guitarists need to get the blood pumping to their muscles before sitting down to practice. How do you warm up before playing? Well, play five bar chords on each string and several scales as fast as you can. You'll notice your hand starts to ache. Let it rest and then start playing.

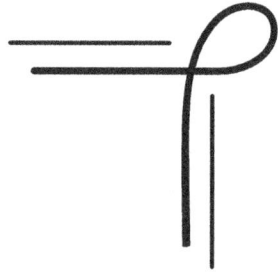

PART 2

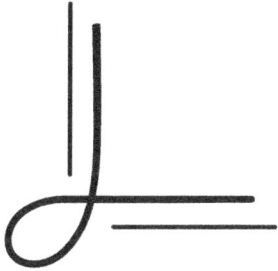

CHAPTER 7

The CAGED System

The CAGED System is, arguably, the simplest way to dominate the guitar fretboard entirely.

Yes, the CAGED System is a compass, a lighthouse for the vast waters of music theory. Moreover, it is so simple that it will surprise that such a modest tool helps you get so much better at playing.

Furthermore, by the time you make it to the end of this book, you'll not only be a better player, but you will also have a much better understanding of your instrument.

I don't want to sound like the protagonist of a Netflix series but, seriously, everything is connected.

What you're about to learn are the ways in which everything is connected and, more importantly, how to use that in your favor.

Yes, learning and mastering the CAGED System has been a pivotal point in my career as a guitarist. I hope I can help you use it so you can unlock the mysteries of our instrument too.

What is the CAGED System?

To begin with, let's define the CAGED System as a map of the fretboard made of five major chords. We're going to learn how to use those (very) basic major chord forms to play any other major chord we need on the fretboard.

Yes, that is, to me at least, the magic of the CAGED System: you learn patterns instead of chords. Therefore, you can use the patterns to play any chord you need anywhere on the fretboard.

Finally, I know what you're thinking and let me tell you (blowing the scoop) that the CAGED System works particularly well with major chords but it is a principle applicable to minor, seventh, and other chords.

Why Should I Learn the CAGED System?

The CAGED System offers a plethora of benefits for players. Let's see some of the most important ones:

» **Learn multiple voicings for a chord** – Chord voicings are the next frontier for guitar players. Yes, it is a concept that piano players work on their entire career and works wonders trying to make your guitar-playing serve the song. For example, if you need to play a G in a very soft section, maybe playing that sixth string is too much. Well, using the CAGED System you can replace that G for a more suitable voicing. That way, you'll still be playing G but results will be better; you'll be serving the song's purpose better.

» **Fretboard visualization** – The guitar's fretboard is a vast canvas to paint beautiful colors on. Yet, it is not a small or easy canvas to learn. On the opposite, there are 6 strings with 12 notes each that, in some guitars appear twice. That gives us at least 100 notes to play on any regular guitar. Yes, you guessed it; the CAGED System works ordering those notes in such a way that, by the time you master it, you will be able to visualize exactly where you want to play your chords at all times.

» **Arpeggios & Soloing** – The CAGED System is not just a system dedicated to chords, it can also be a game-changer when it comes to solos and arpeggios. Furthermore, if you have knowledge about scales, modes, and the CAGED System, you have more tools to choose from than many guitar players. In other words, there's no stopping you; that combined knowledge will give you guitar super powers!

But that's not all; there are many more benefits. For example, when applied to real life, it will help you in these scenarios.

As a songwriter

The CAGED System is a great way to make your compositions more playable choosing the right chord shapes on the right places of the fretboard. In other words, you can just use the most comfortable, closest shapes to play the song's chords and focus on the performance.

For Jams

If you're a guitarist who often goes (or dreams about going) to jams, you'll find the CAGED System a shortcut to guitar mastery and to standing on that stage without playing a single wrong chord or note the entire night.

Playing covers

If you like playing cover songs, you'll find the CAGED System is a way to pick out the chord that's being played in the original and use the most comfortable shape to play it yourself. Also, it will be easier to pick out the chord since, by moving a single shape around the fretboard, you can create any chord; just let your ears guide you.

Introducing the Almighty CAGED System

The CAGED System doesn't receive its name from being sort of a magic cage where you can play your songs. It isn't a scale shape working as a cage either. This system gets its name from an acronym made with the name of five major chords you'll surely know and have played before.

Yes, I'm talking about the C, A, G, E, and D chords:

Understanding Triads

You might have noticed that the chords above have a number or letter on some of the notes. Well, this is because I need to explain a basic music concept: triads.

What are triads? They are a combination of three notes that create a chord. Yes, major and minor chords are triads.

If you stretch to seventh chords, for example, what you have is a triad with an added (seventh) note.

So, CAGED chords are a triad made of:

Root Note + Third + Fifth

To find what notes make each of the chords, we need to go to the scales and count a third and a fifth starting from the chord's root note.

For example, the C major scale offers:

C Major Scale						
I	II	III	IV	V	VI	VII
C	D	E	F	G	A	B

If we take the root (I), the third (III), and the fifth (V), what we get is C – E – G as a triad.

A Major Scale						
I	II	III	IV	V	VI	VII
A	B	C#	D	E	F#	G#

In the case of A, we have A – C# - E as a triad.

G Major Scale						
I	II	III	IV	V	VI	VII
G	A	B	C	D	E	F#

For the G major scale we use G – B – D as a triad.

E Major Scale						
I	II	III	IV	V	VI	VII
E	F#	G#	A	B	C#	D#

For E, the triad is E – G# - B.

D Major Scale						
I	II	III	IV	V	VI	VII
D	E	F#	G	A	B	C#

Finally, the D major scale offers D – F# - A as a triad.

Now, look at the chord diagrams again and find these triads on the fretboard for each of the chords.

Does it make more sense now? Amazing! We're making huge progress here!

What Are The Most-Used Shapes?

Before finishing this chapter, please bear in mind that the three shapes you're more likely to use (the ones that require the less stretching and easiest fingering) are the C, A, and E shapes.

Don't get me wrong, I'm not saying that the others are too complicated, but these are simply simpler to use.

Nevertheless, we're going to learn them all and you'll be making that decision later on.

See you in the next chapter to engage the fun factor, play some more, and take a cool quiz.

CHAPTER 8

Moving the Shapes Around

Now that you're aware of the chords we need to use, it's time for the fun to start!

Yes, we're going to use the CAGED system to cover the entire fretboard. That way, you'll have a better idea of what to do in real-life scenarios with the knowledge you've just acquired.

Finally, at the end of this chapter, you'll find a quiz or questionnaire that will help you assess the knowledge you've learned so far.

Are you ready to unlock the full power of the CAGED system?

Well, go grab your guitar because here we go!

The CAGED System and Your Sixth String, the E Shape

The top three strings on your guitar are doubtlessly the most used ones when playing songs. Therefore, learning how to move the E, A, and D shapes around to create different chords across the fretboard is paramount for a guitar player.

We'll get started with the sixth string first. So, to begin with, we're going to take a look at the available notes on the sixth string.

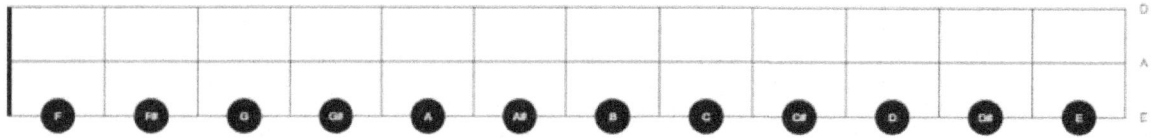

Let's use these notes as a root to create the chords on the 6th string for the entire fretboard. We'll pick several different chords from different keys because you can use the E shape of the CAGED system to find the 7 chords on any key.

For example, if you were playing in the key of C, you would only have natural chords with no accidents (sharps or flats). You could play chords like:

F Major

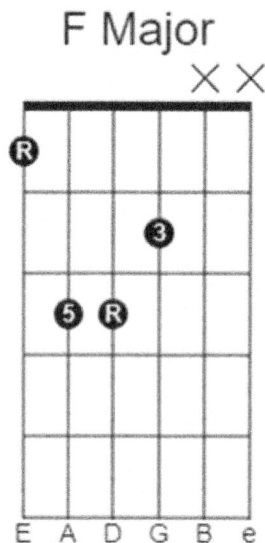

Notice how the same structure of the triad is moved to give us the one we need to form an F major.

Likewise, you could move the same shape up one tone and get a G major that looks like this:

G Major

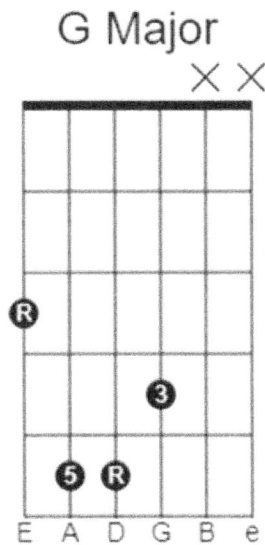

But what if your song wasn't in the key of C but in the key of F# Major; can you play that chord with the E shape? Of course, it looks like this:

F# Major

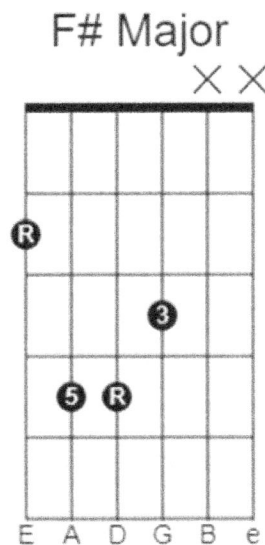

Let's say that your tune follows the I – IV – V chord progression; can you play all three chords using only one shape? Well, of course, that's a piece of cake!

The other two look just like this:

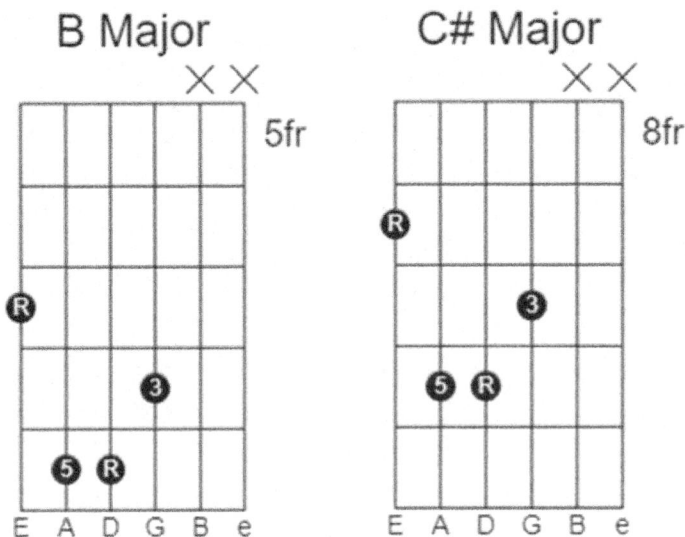

In this case, for example, you can play all three chords of your colossal chorus moving one shape around the neck. Furthermore, this is especially useful for those who sing besides playing the guitar. Yes, moving a single shape around makes it easier to play without looking at the fretboard.

The CAGED System and Your Fifth String, the A Shape

Just like you can move the E shape around and create as many chords as you need with the root on the sixth string, you can also work your way to chord mastery using the fifth string as your root.

Let's take a look at the notes on the fifth string across the fretboard:

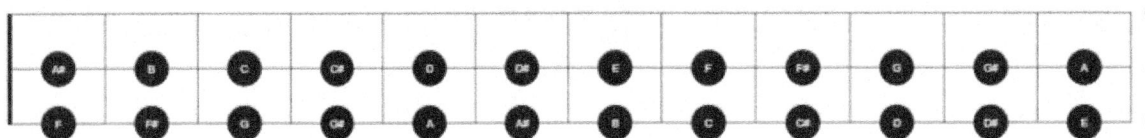

Let's pretend for a minute that you have to create a song using the key of A. Can you form all the chords you need using only the A shape of the CAGED system?

The answer is YES.

For example, if we were to play the quintessential I – IV – V chord progression using only CAGED chords, they would look something like this:

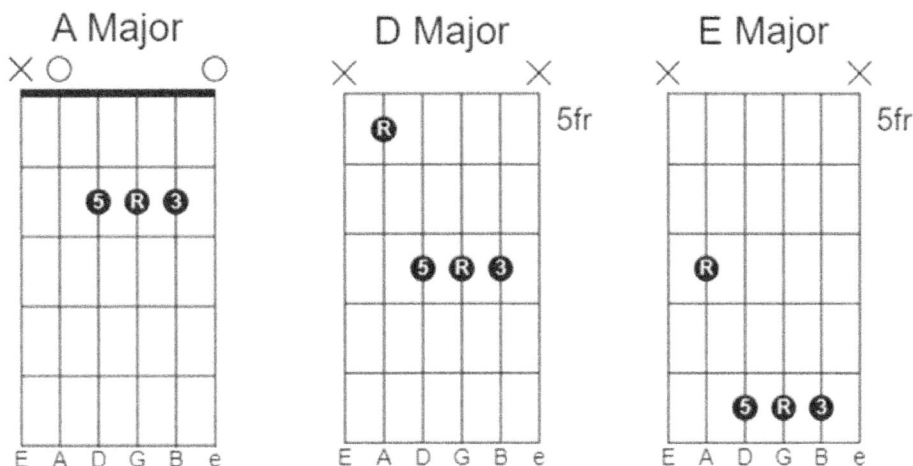

Moreover, let's make it a little more complex by thinking we can do the old Ramones trick and play the same chord progression one tone above for the second verse. We can pivot to our new key, B major, by using a common chord; in this case, E major.

We could play it doing an IV – V – I tandem utilizing the IV degree of the B key, which is E major as a pivotal chord.

Wait, we can do that using the same A shape from the CAGED system to play all chords?

The answer is still YES!

It would look something like this:

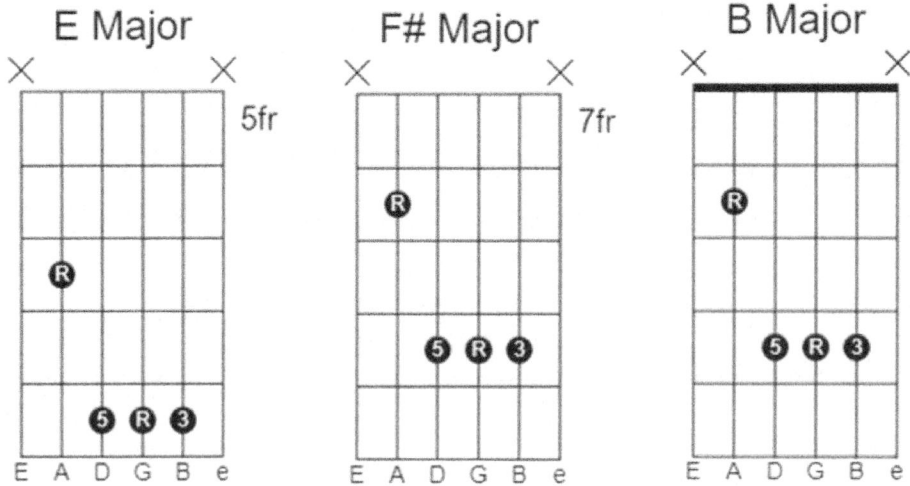

See? We can play the six different chords of a modulated, complex song using a unique shape, the A shape of the CAGED system.

Again, if you're a singer, you can simply move a single shape around and focus on the singing.

The CAGED System and Your Fourth String, the D Shape

This is the last of the shapes we're seeing in this chapter since it completes the trilogy that will help you play 90% of the chords you'll ever need.

We saw that the E shape had the root note on the sixth string, the A shape on the fifth string, and now the D shape on the fourth string.

To begin with, let's complete the notes on the top 3 strings so you can have a full map of how to use these chords across the entire fretboard:

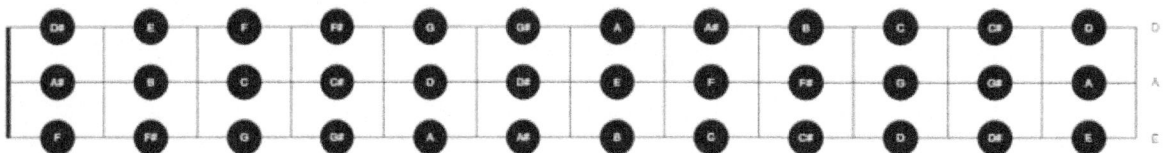

Let's think of a similar exercise to the previous ones but let's center our song around the key of F. To play the most famous formula of all times (I – IV – V), we need F, A#, and C.

Can we make those chords using the D shape only?

You already know the answer.

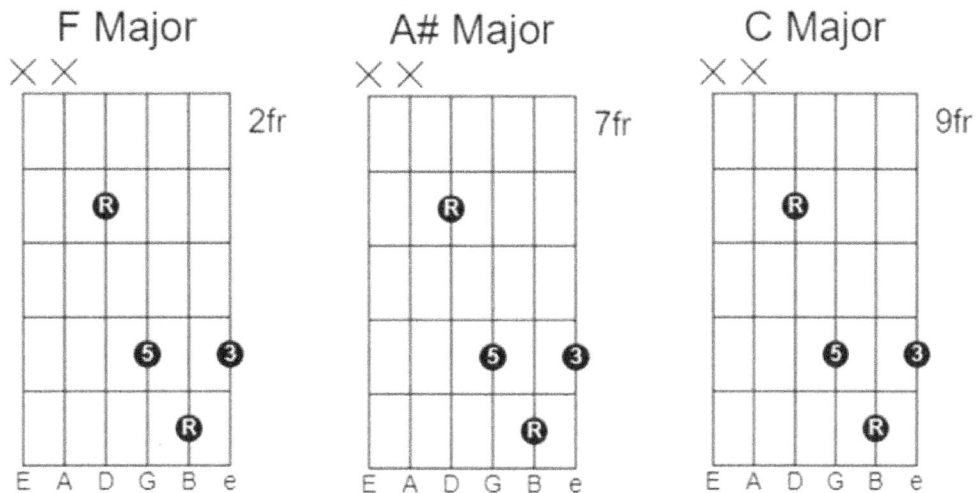

F Major — 2fr

A# Major — 7fr

C Major — 9fr

Let's continue exploring by modulating to a different key. The right move is to find a pivotal chord that can grant us a way into the new key. What if we use C major to move to that scale? Moreover, C major being the V degree of F will sound natural to move to the new I – IV – V structure using it.

The chords we need are C, F, and G. We already have two out of three; the only one we need to put together using the CAGED system's D shape is G major.

G Major

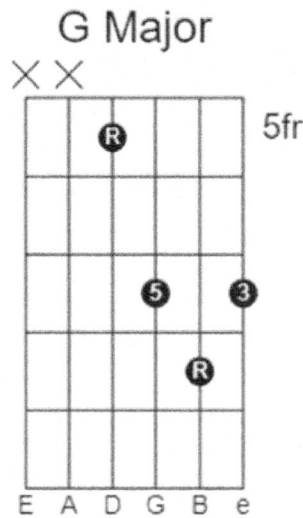

So, to finish this chapter, let's just pour all we've learned with our new shapes into three easy-to-play and super fun exercises.

Go get your guitar because there's a *whole lotta playing goin' on!*

Exercise 1 – Sixth String

Exercise 2 – Fifth String

Exercise 3 – Fourth String

Exercise 4 – The Ultimate Mix-up!

Now that you've played all the chords in every CAGED position, let's try an exercise in which we mix these positions, open, and bar chord shapes so you can get a better grasp of CAGED chords' true power unleashed.

To make it simpler, we'll use two keys with no accidents that you can pivot back and forth from: C major and A minor (its relative minor).

The exercise starts with minor bar chords which gives it a gloomy atmosphere you can think of as the verse. The inclusion of a full bar chord is because playing the sixth string makes it darker which is exactly what you need to put the audience into "verse mode".

By the fifth bar, the progression moves to the III degree of the A minor scale (which is also the I degree of the C major scale) using a CAGED shape on the fifth string. That shape is followed by F and G played with CAGED shapes on the fourth string. This adds flavor and texture because are unusual shapes.

By the time you get to bar 9, you'll need to play F and G again but in the E shape of the CAGED system. Bar 10 utilizes a seventh bar chord to accentuate tension and make room for our almighty chorus.

Speaking of which, the chorus resolves the tension playing the I chord of C major in the open position. You'll notice a sensation of "openness" with that simple change. That chord is followed by the IV and V degrees (F and G) played with full bar chords to keep the epic sensation of the open C major going.

Finally, the exercise ends on the same chord it started modulating back to the original key of A minor.

Key Takeaways of the Exercise

Let's take a look at the main takeaways of this exercise.

» **Dynamics** – Using different shapes to play the same chords is working on dynamics. This keeps a simple chord progression interesting. If you were to play the same exercise using only open chords, the result will be very different (try it and see it for yourself!)

» **Moods** – The inclusion of minor and seventh chords together with major chords helps the progression set a mood. You can clearly hear the difference between bars 1 to 4 and 11 to 14.

» **Movement Economy** – Throughout the exercise we not only chose the chords to play but also where to play them to make it more comfortable to move from one to the next. A good example of this is the C major with CAGED shape A and F and G major with CAGED shape D.

To wrap up this chapter, I'm going to leave you a personal present just because I'm very proud you made it this far with me and because you practiced last exercise a lot to make it sound awesome.

This is a map of the fretboard in which every shape is connected to the last. This is, the exact way that the CAGED system covers the entire fretboard.

Use it, learn it, and let it grow on you. Before you know, you'll navigate the entire fretboard easily with your eyes closed.

CHAPTER 9

A Few Extra Chords

We have already established more than once the importance of dynamics for guitar players and songwriters. Yes, dynamics are what keep a listener engaged because they don't know what's coming up next.

This is not a random occurrence or a magic trick; on the contrary, we can make it happen.

How can we make it happen? Well, by broadening our musical vocabulary and including different chords.

That's exactly what's coming up next: we're going to add 10 new chords to your arsenal. You'll not only have more fun playing but your compositions will also be more engaging, interesting, and beautiful.

Go get your guitar because there's a lot of playing to do!

Major Seventh Chords (Maj7)

I know what you're thinking; this guy is wrong, we've seen seventh chords already! Well, let me tell you that this old guitar man has a trick or two up his sleeve.

In this chapter, we're going to add two more flavors to the seventh chords we've already seen.

Dominant Seventh vs. Major Seventh

The seventh chords we've seen in chapter 6 are called dominant 7th chords and add steroids to the dominant chord's feeling of urgency.

The formula for those chords is the root note, a third, a fifth, and the seventh lowered a half step (AKA a flat seventh). For example, if we pour the C scale into that formula, what we get is:

$$C (I) + E (III) + G (V) + Bb (VIIb)$$

What happens if, instead of lowering the seventh half a step, we use it as is? Well, the result is a maj7 chord that's sonically different. The formula looks like this:

$$C (I) + E (III) + G (V) + B (VII)$$

Let's put these chords into diagrams so you can hear the difference as you play them:

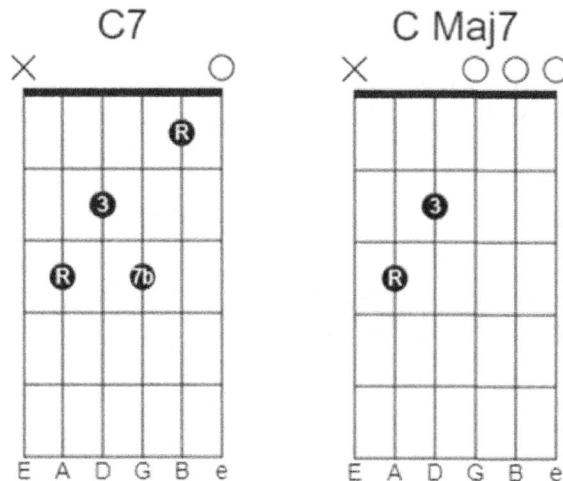

What difference does this make sonically to play either of these chords? Well, the dominant seventh chord is a minor seventh on top of a major chord. This creates a sonic struggle between major and minor that generates the famous tension we've been talking about for several chapters.

The major seventh chords, on the other hand, are a simple I + III + V + VII formula that sounds beautiful without the tension. Yes, it is a single note of difference, but the chord changes completely.

Major Seventh across the Fretboard

Let's use bar chords (or the closest to in the first case) to create the CMaj7 chord with a root on the sixth and fifth strings. Knowing these shapes and the root, you can create any Maj7 chord you need on the fretboard.

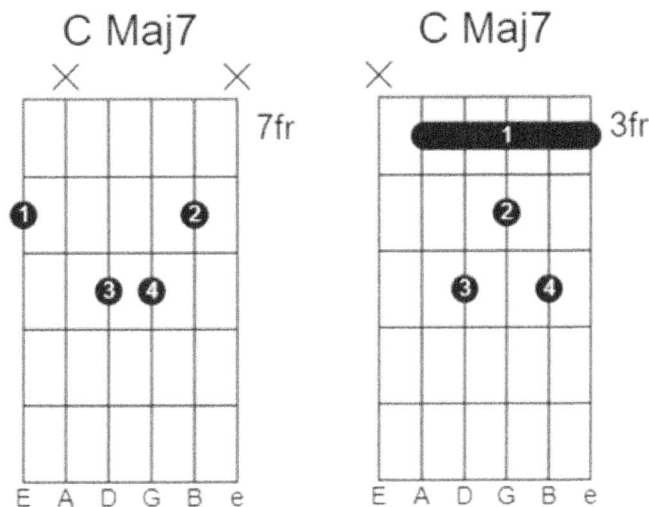

Finally, let's clear out something that generates confusion in many of my students. If you see CMaj7 it doesn't mean it is a C major with a seventh note added. It means it is a C major with a major seventh added. In other words, instead of thinking of the chord as CMaj + 7, you need to think of it as a C + Maj7.

Minor Seventh Chords (m7)

At the beginning of this book, we talked about major and minor chords. By now, you surely know that major and minor chords are triads (AKA chords with three notes). You also know these triads are the base for other chords, like dominant and major seventh chords.

But what happens if, instead of starting with a major triad, we start with a minor triad?

That's right! Adding a seventh to a minor triad will give us a minor seventh chord.

Before we move on to the formula and the shapes let me tell you that minor seventh chords are very powerful. Indeed, they are loaded with an immense amount of emotion that can cause any composition to turn blue immediately.

In a nutshell, make sure you don't overuse them.

That being said, when putting together the previous seventh chords we were borrowing our notes from the major scale. To put together a minor seventh chord, we need to borrow from the minor scale.

So, for example, if we take the scale of A minor and pour it into our formula, what we get is this:

A (I) – C (III) – E (V) – G (VII)

Translating that to an open-position chord, what we get is this:

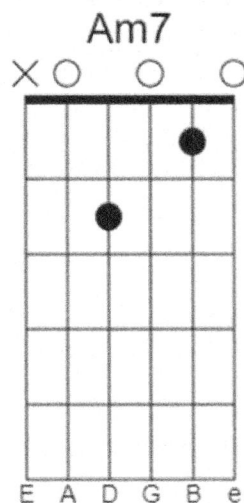

By now, you know that we can transform an open position chord into a bar chord and move it around (remember the CAGED system, right?). Therefore, if we wanted to transform this Am7 into a Bm7, we should move the same structure one tone up and bar the open notes.

What you get is this:

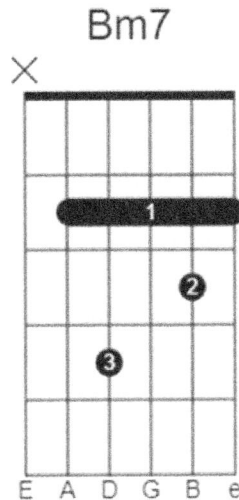

Can we make minor seventh chords with the root on the sixth string? Well, the answer is yes, we have to repeat the same notes but starting on the top string of your guitar.

Using the Am7 formula, the result looks like this:

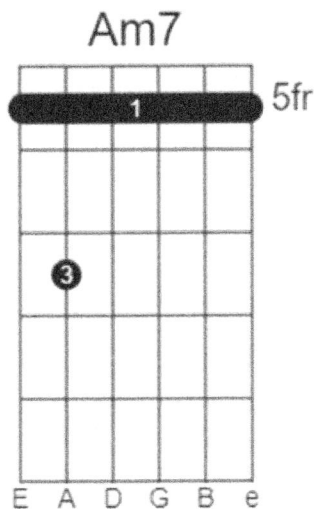

Moving these shapes around, you can create any minor seventh chord you want across the fretboard.

Suspended Chords (Sus2 & Sus4)

Perhaps, the title made you feel a little panic because it sounds epic, jazzy, and, of course, complicated. Yet, that couldn't be further from the truth. These chords are great to add a breath of fresh air to a common chord and bring some light to a chord progression.

Yes, suspended chords aren't only easy to learn and play; they can also help you add life and bright colors to any song.

But why are they called "suspended" chords?

Well, it's like a sports game, one of the three notes in the triad of a chord gets sent off the pitch (suspended) and replaced with another note.

The suspended note is always the third (major or minor) and replaced with the note indicated in the name of the chord. In the case of a Sus2 chord, the third is replaced with a second. Likewise, in the case of a Sus4 chord, the third is replaced with a fourth.

What? Do you mean that's all there is to know about Sus2 and Sus4 chords? Yes, there are no hidden mysteries or tricks, they are as easy as it gets.

Let's use my favorite key to demonstrate these chords: D (it even looks like a smile, D is a great key).

The formula for a Dsus2 chord is:

$$D \text{ (I)} + E \text{ (II)} + A \text{ (V)}$$

The chord looks something like this:

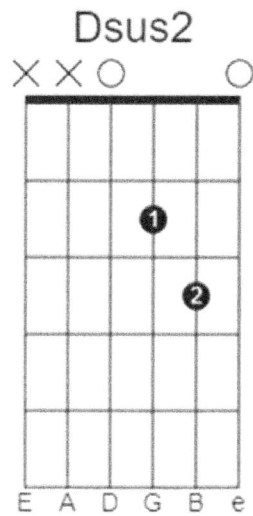

Dsus2

Following the same line, a Dsus4 follows this formula:

D (I) + G (IV) + A (V)

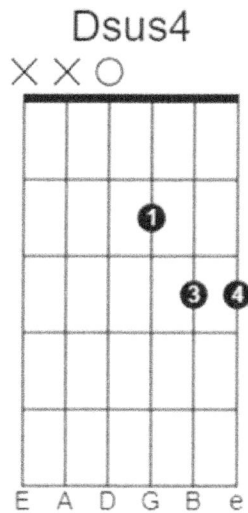

Dsus4

Can you take these chords and transform them into the chords you need anywhere on the fretboard? Well, of course, you already know how to do that because of the CAGED system.

This is what Esus2 and Esus4 look like:

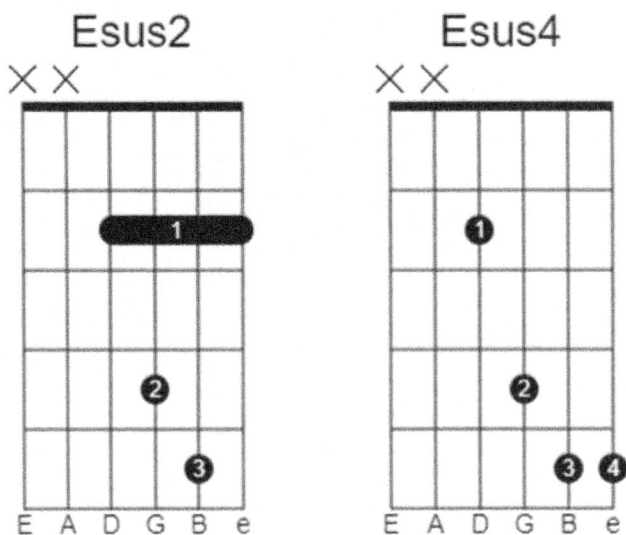

Can we take the same principle and apply it to a bar chord on the fifth string? Well, of course, we can; we have to begin our journey from an A major chord and then turn it into a Sus2 and a Sus4.

This is what they look like:

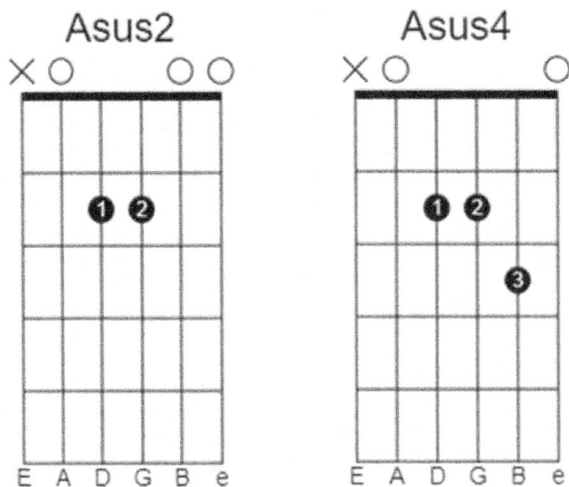

Let's turn this into a Bsus2 and a Bsus4 with what we learned in the CAGED system.

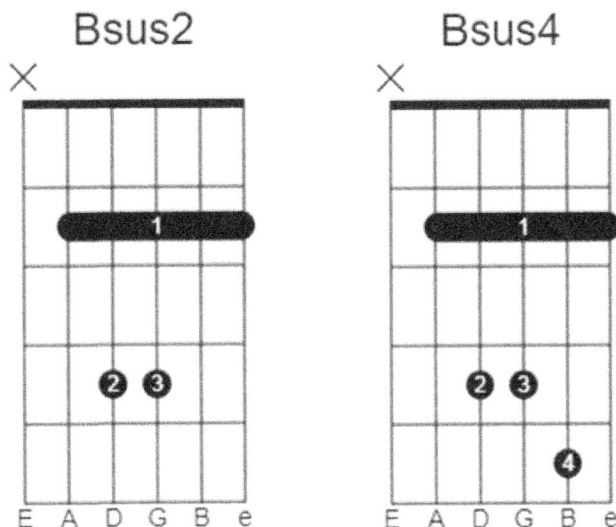

Let's do a very small and easy exercise so you can learn how to use the Bsus2 and Bsus4 to embellish an otherwise very common B major chord.

Before wrapping up suspended chords, and in case you were wondering about it since the triad isn't complete (the third is suspended, with a long face, sitting on the bench), the sus2 and sus4 chords aren't considered either minor or major.

Dominant Seventh Suspended 4 Chords (7sus4)

We made it to the last of the new chords you're about to learn to broaden and embellish your guitar vocabulary. This chord is a combination of other chords we've seen in this same chapter and a chord we saw in chapter 6.

Yes, we're going to take away some of the tension from the dominant seventh chord by removing the clash between major and minor that makes them want to resolve to the root so desperately.

Instead, we're going to give these chords a different flavor that'll ease the transition.

We're doing this with our trusty C major scale so we can avoid sharps and flats but don't worry because you'll learn to play them all over the fretboard on the fifth and sixth strings.

So, to get started, we know that the C7 chord follows this formula:

C (I) + E (III) + G (V) + Bb (bVII)

To transform any chord to a sus4 chord, we need to replace the third with the fourth. To reach it, we need to move a half-step above the third.

Therefore, C7sus4 follows this formula:

C (I) + F (IV) + G (V) + Bb (bVII)

If we translate this formula to our fretboard, we can come up with many shapes. These are the ones that we'll find with the sixth and fifth string bar chords *(or the closest possible)*.

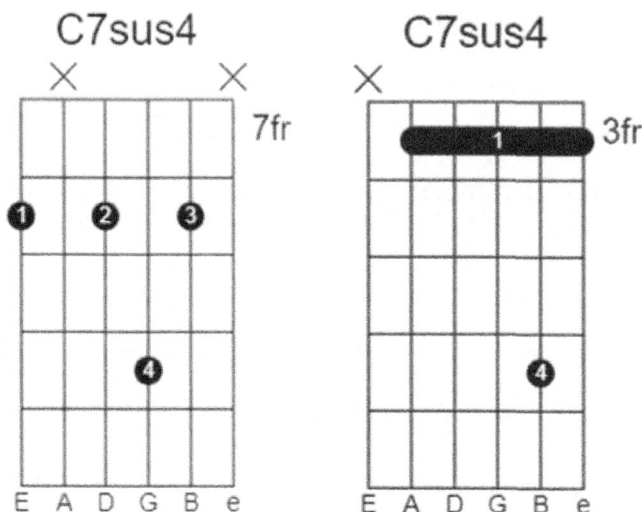

Since sus4 chords aren't technically major or minor, feel free to experiment with these chords and use them where you'll normally use a major or minor dominant seventh chord.

CHAPTER 10

Bar Chords Across the Genres

The first thing to say to begin this chapter is congratulations; you're a tiny step away from mastering not only bar chords, but chords in general.

Yet, before we wrap this up, you're going to practice everything you've just learned by playing fun progressions that cover a plethora of musical styles. This way, you shall be prepared for whatever your musical life throws at you.

Never mind what the path brings, once you finish this chapter, you'll be ready for it.

Speaking of which, go get your guitar, stretch your fingers, and let's get down to business because there's a whole lot of playing to do.

1. R&B

Rhythm and Blues or R&B is a musical style that has gotten a lot of attention lately. Artists like Alicia Keys, Bruno Mars, Mary J Blige, and Anderson Paak made it to the mainstream by utilizing the style's characteristic syncopated beat to build monster melodies.

This musical style is played on guitar using small shapes on the higher register to make room for mammoth bass lines that carry the groove. So, pay close attention to the choice of chords and also where we chose to play them.

Also, pay attention to the tempo and play it using a metronome respecting the 6/8 time signature. The tempo is set at 90. Nevertheless, feel free to start slower and speed it up if you want.

Finally, make sure you respect the rests to get the rhythm going so you can set the dance floor on fire.

Oh, and before we start; you'll need to play a chord we haven't seen in the book: G# diminished (G#°).

Here's the diagram:

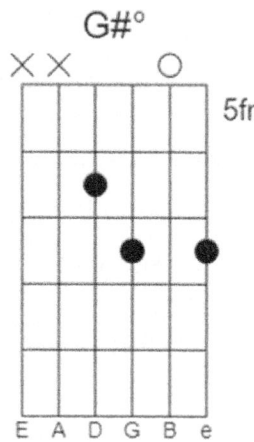

2. Bossa Nova

Bossa Nova is a music style born in Brazil, South America. It's derived from samba but takes the focus away from percussion and puts it on melody. Also, it is a juxtaposition of genres since the complexity of the compositions can be thought of as closer to jazz.

That being said, bossa nova is a dancing style; therefore, it's meant to make people move. Perhaps you've heard hits like "Garota do Ipanema" by Antonio Carlos Jobim and Vinicius de Moraes. If you did, you know what I'm talking about; your body moves by itself!

But how does this musical style achieve the perfect balance between emotion and fun? Well by adding seventh and minor seventh chords to a rhythm pattern that makes you move.

Yes, pay close attention to these emotional chords and respect the rhythm pattern and you'll witness this phenomenon yourself too. Just don't blame me if you spend the next following week singing bossa hits!

Oh, in case you're thinking that the note left outside the ties is a mistake, think again; you have to play it to keep the rhythm going.

3. Pop

Unlike bossa nova, pop is a genre that doesn't need any introduction at all. Moreover, the category keeps getting bigger and bigger as the years go by. Nowadays, you can find hip-hop, R&B, rock, and even dance artists being considered pop.

The one thing that makes them belong to this category, though, is the fact that they are popular and many people like them. How to make the world like your music? Well, although there are no sure recipes, we can say that, for starters, you have to make beautiful music and hide a hook or two inside.

For this exercise, we created an easygoing chord progression that works perfectly with the particular rhythm pattern we chose. As you strum along, make sure you pay attention to the rests and also the figures; that's what gives the progression the hook.

Finally, notice how you can end a progression with a huge statement using open-position chords. Yes, the whole thing goes from huge to epic on that final strum (if you close your eyes, you can hear the arena calling your name already!).

4. Jazz

Jazz is a musical style some players feel can get a little too complicated and might cause them to refrain from practicing it. Although it is true that most jazz compositions are complex, it is a musical style that allows for minimalism too.

Moreover, in this exercise, we'll practice the "Charleston" rhythm pattern, one of the most legendary and common in this musical style.

Finally, before we start it's important that you know that sometimes less is more in jazz, that's why the rhythm figures are so minimalistic. Just set the tempo slow and focus on landing every note at the correct spot.

5. Eagles

The Eagles are a rock n roll band that has left a mark in the history of music by crafting amazing songs. Yes, I'm sure you've heard "Hotel California" before. Well, that song alone sold over 28 million copies in the USA, and more than 32 million worldwide.

What was the recipe behind the success?

Well, we can begin by saying they found a way of creating compelling chord progressions to lay an epic melody on. That's exactly what we did for you in the following chord progression. Furthermore, in this exercise, we added the strumming pattern with the down and upstrokes (V and ∧ respectively).

So, make sure you respect rhythm figures and strumming patterns to get that quintessential on-the-road sing-along groove going.

Bb   F   Gm   A⁷

6. Cat Stevens

Mr. Cat Stevens or Yusuf Islam is a US-born singer-songwriter that amazed the world with hits such as "The First Cut is the Deepest", "Wild World", and "Father and Son" among many others.

What makes Cat Stevens different from all the other singer-songwriters of his time? Well, besides his obvious talent as a lyricist and songwriter, he could play beautiful chord progressions with a rhythmic pattern that was engaging enough to do solo performances.

That's exactly what we're about to do here using chords you know well and that work amazingly well together.

Finally, pay close attention to the way B7 in the end raises the tension to resolve back to Em.

Em   Am   D   G   C   Am   B⁷

7. Jazz

This second jazz exercise starts with dual extra-mellow whole-note chords and then moves on to a repeating pattern. Notice how the rests create accents that give the chord progression a sort of push forward.

Finally, by the time you exit the repeated section, the following two chords can work as the perfect bridge to go somewhere else and continue playing. Furthermore, the last chord being a dominant seventh gives the ending of the exercise a sense of urgency that demands to be resolved, and soon.

8. Variation

This is a variation of the last exercise. In this case, after you exit the repeated section, the combination of chords played once each at the last bar can give the progression the final touch it needs to leave the audience in awe.

So, pay close attention to rests and chord combinations, especially on the last bar.

9. Pop

As we said before, pop can feed from a multiplicity of different styles to create catchy melodies and make great sing-along songs.

In this case, the first part of the progression is based on sharp chords which give it a sense of urgency pushing the song forward. We can take advantage of this as players with our rhythm pattern choice. In this case, the combination of quarter and eighth notes make it easygoing and uplifting.

By the second part of the exercise (the second repeating section), the inclusion of chords such as Bm and E major anchor the composition into a chorus-like section that can work wonders with a beautiful melody on top.

10. Rock n Suspended Roll

We made it to the final exercise. In this case, what we have is a very uplifting first section (rocking if you add a little overdrive to your electric six-stringer) followed by a section that could work as a bridge or a verse.

Notice how the suspended chords change the mood of an otherwise super-simple chord progression with a repeating D chord. Also, notice how, when you add the sixth string to the equation, the mood turns a little darker and the progression grows.

Finally, the final succession of chords leads the entire composition to the final diminished chord that can resolve to the tonic bringing back our uplifting chorus.

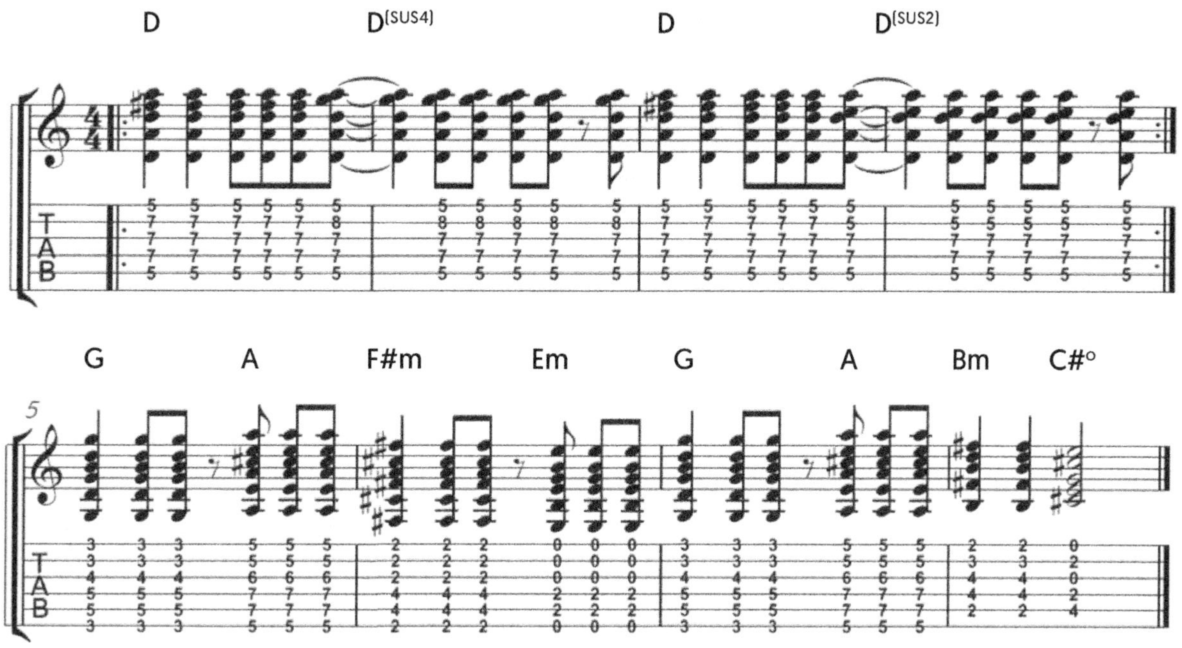
D
D(SUS4)
D
D(SUS2)
TAB
G
A
F#m
Em
G
A
Bm
C#°
5
TAB

Final Words

Well, it's been quite a ride, hasn't it?

We surely played more than a handful of bar chords in every position imagined. Furthermore, I taught you the almighty CAGED system for you to master the entire fretboard. But that wasn't all; you also learned chords that can create different textures, capable of taking your compositions from amateur to professional-sounding. Finally, we dissected some of the main music styles and applied everything we learned to play each of them.

Yes, I have to say I poured most of my secrets into the pages of this book.

By now, you should be able to play any chord anywhere you want on the fretboard. Moreover, you should also be able to navigate through different chords to create your own, amazing music.

I just want to say that I'm very proud of you, your efforts, and the road we have come together. You practiced hard, pushed through the frustration, and here you are, a master of your own sonic universe.

As a piece of advice from someone who has over 20 years of experience in this business, continue to expand your musical vocabulary; learn new chords, textures, flavors, and colors. Keep on learning new songs, dissect them, keep it interesting, and never forget to have fun.

After all, that's the main reason all of us picked up the instrument in the first place, right?

Play hard, enjoy a lot, and let the world fall in love with the beautiful music pouring out of you.

Thank you for reading and happy playing!

Farewell

Pssssttt....

What are you doing here? Are you lost?

Do people even look at the last pages of a book?

Jokes aside, I hope you enjoyed this book. I certainly loved the process of writing it.

If you enjoyed this book, could you take 2 minutes to leave a review about it?

Reviews are the lifeblood for small publishers and help us get our books into the hands of more guitarists like you.

We read every review personally and appreciate each one of it.

To leave a review, simply go to the platform you purchased the book from and type in your review.

With that said, here's Guitar Head signing off!

Until next time then? I'll see you in another book.

The End

Printed in Great Britain
by Amazon

38258857R00073